Just Breathe

CHOOSING JOY, ONE BREATH AT A TIME

Leanne Waterworth

WESTBOW
PRESS®
A DIVISION OF THOMAS NELSON
& ZONDERVAN

This book is a work of non-fiction. Unless otherwise noted, the author
and the publisher make no explicit guarantees as to the accuracy of
the information contained in this book and in some cases, names of
people and places have been altered to protect their privacy.

THE HOLY BIBLE, NEW INTERNATIONAL VERSION®,
NIV® Copyright © 1973, 1978, 1984, 2011 by Biblica, Inc.®
Used by permission. All rights reserved worldwide.

Scripture taken from The Message. Copyright © 1993, 1994, 1995, 1996,
2000, 2001, 2002. Used by permission of NavPress Publishing Group.

WestBow Press books may be ordered through booksellers or by contacting:

WestBow Press
A Division of Thomas Nelson & Zondervan
1663 Liberty Drive
Bloomington, IN 47403
www.westbowpress.com
1 (866) 928-1240

Because of the dynamic nature of the Internet, any web addresses or
links contained in this book may have changed since publication and
may no longer be valid. The views expressed in this work are solely those
of the author and do not necessarily reflect the views of the publisher,
and the publisher hereby disclaims any responsibility for them.

Any people depicted in stock imagery provided by Thinkstock are models,
and such images are being used for illustrative purposes only.
Certain stock imagery © Thinkstock.

ISBN: 978-1-5127-7109-1 (sc)
ISBN: 978-1-5127-7111-4 (hc)
ISBN: 978-1-5127-7110-7 (e)

Library of Congress Control Number: 2017900125

Print information available on the last page.

WestBow Press rev. date: 01/18/2017

Contents

Psalm 150:6 NIV, *"Let everything that has breath praise the Lord!"*

THIS BOOK IS DEDICATED TO:

THE COUNTLESS CF SUPERHEROES WHO HAVE
ENCOURAGED AND STRENGTHENED US ALONG
THIS INCREDIBLE JOURNEY. WHETHER YOU
BROUGHT US A MEAL, CYCLED FOR LIFE, CLIMBED
STAIRS, MADE A DONATION, VOLUNTEERED
OR KEPT US IN PRAYER; YOU ARE ALL HEROES
TO OUR FAMILY. MAY YOU BE ENCOURAGED TO
KNOW THAT YOUR WORK PLEASES THE LORD.

Hebrews 6:10, *"God is not unjust; He will not forget
your work and the love you have shown Him as you
have helped His people and continue to help them."*

ACKNOWLEDGEMENTS

First and foremost, I want to recognize my husband and hero Nathan: You have supported and encouraged me every step of the way – even when my nose was forever stuck in a laptop and I suggested pizza for supper; again. I couldn't have done this without you.

My children, Carson, Ella and Anders: For allowing me to share your stories in the hope that it will help and inspire others. I am proud to be your mom.

Dr. Melissa L. Hall MD, my trusted physician and friend: You have been with our family through every chapter of this book. I am so grateful for your presence, wisdom, and friendship.

The St. Croix Regional Medical Center: For providing excellent medical expertise within a small community. We appreciate the care and advice we have received over many years.

Our CF Care Team at the University of Minnesota Masonic Children's Hospital: I know our boys are in the most capable and qualified hands.

The entire community of St. Croix Falls, WI: We are eternally grateful for how you have come along side us through the ups and downs. It truly does take a village to raise a family, and we feel blessed that our town is filled with such loving and compassionate people.

Our diligent and noble friends of the Cystic Fibrosis Foundation:

Thank you for working tirelessly to raise awareness and funds so that one day CF will stand for Cure Found!

Angeline Joy Semmens: Her brave battle with colon cancer inspired me to choose joy in the midst of the most difficult circumstances.

Deborah Spreng, Julie Barnhill, Rachel Riebe, Rita Platt, Jana Greg and Angie Gorres: For sharing your editing expertise and advice. You stretched and encouraged me and I am so grateful.

And finally, to my parents, Steve and Carolann Rosenthal, and Jon and Marie Waterworth: You have cared for us in such an intimate way; shedding tears, making meals, learning medical treatments, and experiencing our highs and lows. Your support and devotion has given us strength and we thank God for you.

August 1, 2014, approximately 2:00 PM; Belleview Road, Choteau Montana:

I didn't feel physically ready to begin a mile run. My clothes were soaked through and water still dripped from my shirt. My legs were covered in mud and blood; my feet were bare, having lost my shoes in the accident. My turf was a rocky, gravel road in Western Montana. It stretched out between me and the nearest house, covered in sharp mountain rocks, baking in the hot afternoon sun. I hadn't even started and I was already gasping for breath. Some of it was from shock after just being in a serious van wreck. But some of it was exhaustion from wading through deep water, pulling and helping people to safety. I shivered in the ninety-degree heat. In normal circumstances, it would have been ridiculous to consider going for a run. I was from Wisconsin and not accustomed to the thin mountain air. But these were not normal circumstances. And no amount of athletic training could have prepared me for it.

People needed rescuing, including my seven-year-old son and I was the only one who could go. As my physical body screamed "no!" my emotional state said, "go!" Yes, there was pain in my neck, legs and arms. My lungs burned in protest. The gravel tore through the tender flesh on my feet; rocks embedding in them. It would take weeks to get them all out. But my adrenaline was so revved up, there was nothing stopping me.

The events that brought me up to this point were remarkable alone. Now add in this unbelievable twist and I felt like I must be dreaming; certainly a nightmare! We were on vacation after all. How could this happen? Yet, intense agony and a struggle to breathe as I ran down a lonely stretch of road kept me very much aware that this was indeed happening. "God please help me!"

A Word Before...

I was fifteen years old when I first saw my husband. He was sixteen at the time. It was Wednesday night youth group and I was the new girl in town. I sat in the bleachers watching kids play basketball while a girl named Laurie pointed out the names of different students to me. One boy in a sleeveless T-shirt captured my attention and I kept asking what his name was.

"I already told you," Laurie snickered. "That's Nathan, the youth pastor's son." She caught me. And if I wasn't careful I was probably gawking too. After all, he was tall, blond, tan and athletic. Nathan was a grade above me. As he moved around the court effortlessly I considered my chances of becoming a high school basketball cheerleader, even though I currently home-schooled.

A few months later I invited my best friend Sara to youth group and pointed out Nathan to her. "See? That's him. That's the guy I'm going to marry someday."

She looked at me incredulously and said, "Leanne, he doesn't even know your name." She was right. I was no Guess Jeans kind of girl, but I did have my totally awesome permed hair and skillfully styled bangs held firmly in place with Aqua Net going for me.

"I'll let you be my maid of honor at our wedding." I fought off her negativity with the incentive.

"Alright you've got a deal." She replied. Five years later I kept my promise to her.

Obviously, I had no idea what I was getting into as a fifteen-year-old girl when I fell head over heels for Nathan. When I first saw him, it was the external things that drew me to him; his outward appearance, athleticism and confidence. I didn't really know what love was; not really; not fully.

When Nathan did finally take notice of me, our early dating years were a blast with snowmobiling in the winter and fishing in the summer. We both worked at the same flower shop in town and went to the same college after high school graduation. However, it wasn't the fun dates, flowers, letters or jewelry that solidified my commitment to him.

Nathan was eighteen years old when his parents, Jon and Marie, took in a newborn foster daughter named Stephanie. But she quickly became something uniquely special to everyone and when his parents were considering the idea of adoption he told them, "If you don't adopt this girl, I will."

That was when I knew my future forever with Nathan was sealed. He had the heart of gold I wanted, and ultimately needed. I know some people thought we were crazy for getting married at the young age of twenty and twenty-one. To this day I have no regrets about it. We knew what we had was good, so why wait?

But it would take years to truly understand just how good. ...

Holidays, babies, job loss, a new house, disease, new friends, death, tragedy and travels... These experiences, both exciting and difficult, would test and try us. However, in the end they always made us stronger; praise God!

Through it all, Nathan has been a provider, protector, father, caretaker, sacrificial giver, my rock, cheerleader, loving husband, and faithful friend. I didn't see all of that from the bleachers as a fifteen-year-old girl. Or even at the altar, when I said, "I do, in good times and bad, in sickness and in health," in front of 375 guests. I'm thankful God gave me a partner like Nathan as we continue to journey through here, one foot in front of the other, one breath at a time.

Chapter 1

THE JOURNEY BEGINS

With a marriage license and college under our belts, my husband Nathan and I felt we had a bright future ahead of us. An older mentor couple from our church joked that we now belonged to the D.I.N.K.'s club: Double Income No Kids. Nathan and I relished our early twenties by living and working in downtown St. Paul. We rented a decent apartment that had a nicely sized indoor pool, hot tub, tanning salon, and workout facility. We ate out several times a week, indulged in some traveling, and even participated in a mission trip to China. Life was good and we were enjoying it. Sometimes though, I actually felt guilty about how well things were going for us. At that time, we had family and friends who were struggling with various trials like unemployment and the loss of a child. I questioned why God would allow Nathan and me to experience such blessings while other good Christian people were suffering through adversities. It didn't make sense to me. And then our pastor preached a sermon that seemed to answer some of my deep questions. Ric Stanghelle of Lakes Free Church shared with his congregation how we will all go through periods of blessings and hardships during the course of our lives, and they're not necessarily based on works or behavior. When those times of prosperity come, we shouldn't feel guilty. Instead, acknowledge where those blessings come from, *enjoy* them, *share them* and most important, *thank* God! Especially since at some point, we know we'll experience the hard times as well. That's how life is here on earth; filled with ups and downs. But one thing we can be sure of is that God will be with us through them all.

Pastor Ric's words put me at ease, although admittedly I didn't really want to ponder the kinds of trials I might someday have to face. Up to that point, I'd had a pretty normal life. I was raised by a loving family. I'd never lost anyone close to me. No car accidents, natural disasters, fires, or diseases. But I did take his advice and thanked God for our jobs, health, and the possibility of starting a family someday. And I prayed and offered help to our friends and relatives who were in the trenches.

Nathan and I decided to wait several years before having children. But that didn't mean we disliked kids. We actually both loved them and invested many volunteer hours a week with our church's youth group and teaching Sunday school. We also had fun imagining what it would be like to raise our own sweet bundle of joy one day. Who would they look like? Would we have boys or girls? We looked forward to all sorts of things like watching them take their first steps or playing baseball with them in the back yard. We imagined teaching them to ride bikes or learning how to catch fish. Of course we didn't necessarily consider realities in parenthood like discovering a toddler who just smeared his diaper contents all over the living room floor, walls, furniture, and kitchen appliances. I didn't expect to one day call security because our young daughter was lost in a busy shopping mall. And I certainly *never* imagined my five-year-old would consider unbuckling his seat belt and opening his car door, falling from the vehicle, while I was still driving! A trip to the doctor revealed no serious injuries- just some terrible abrasions and a very devastated mother.

I thought I wanted a large family like my remarkable little Italian grandma did. She and my grandpa raised six children in a tiny house with only one bathroom. She was also a full-time nurse for thirty years. I contemplated that career path myself for about one minute. But I didn't like the sight of blood, puke, poop or mucus. Little did I realize that when I eventually became a mother, the title automatically included in-home nurse and I would experience all four of those bodily fluids in the same hour! It is truly amazing what those babies can expel out of their adorable little bodies. But I think it's interesting that God gives us what we need *when* we need it. Sure, I puked into the bathtub as I tried to scoop out the poop my baby had so nicely left for me to clean up. The important part is that I survived the ordeal.

God ultimately gave me and my husband three bleach-blond, blue-eyed, lightly freckled children. When they are together smiling, they make the cutest family portrait; if only it were that easy. As an inexperienced parent I had no idea what a feat it would be to get all three children to sit still, and *not* touch each other or aggravate, fart, moo like a cow, spit up, sing, knock over the back drop, pick their nose, cross their eyes or cry during a photograph session! But I was wrong. I now fully participate in pinching, threatening and if I have to, bribing my children when their pictures are being taken. Because sadly, even with age, it is still just as difficult to get them to cooperate for the camera.

Ella, Carson and Anders; summer 2015.
Photo by Amy Colleen Photography

Carson is our firstborn. Then twenty-two months later our vivacious daughter Ella Pearl arrived, followed by Anders who came two and a half years after that. Everywhere we go people tell us they look so much alike. But their personalities are uniquely different, it's remarkable. One way I like to describe them is this: Picture all three of my kids playing with a bouncy ball at a school playground when suddenly a mean kid comes and steals their ball.

Carson would passively just let them take it saying, "I guess you can have the ball. I didn't really want to play anyway."

Ella, on the other hand, would confidently tell the bully, "Hey, that's not very nice! If you don't return our ball I'm going to tell on you."

And Anders would boldly push up his sleeves and announce, "Give that ball back or I'll punch you in the face!"

To me, this is a comical but fitting explanation. Carson is gentle, cautious and on the shy side. Ella is confident, a caregiver and a leader. And Anders is courageous, a fighter and full of energy. I love their differences and am excited to see them continue to grow and change.

Raising children has been such an incredible privilege and unique example for me of creation. To witness God taking traits from both me and Nathan and intricately weaving each child into exactly what He wants them to be is a blessing. Nathan and I stand firm in the belief that God created each and every person with purpose and intent. He doesn't make mistakes. Not ever.

This is my family's journey. ...

The Polar Vortex of 2012-13 felt particularly harsh for our family. Carson was ten at the time, Ella eight and Anders six. It wasn't just because it arrived early and lasted until May, plaguing us with record amounts of snow. We even had a blizzard, requiring a school closure on April 1; talk about an April fool's joke! I'm not exactly one who appreciates this time of year. I call our neck of the woods in St. Croix Falls, Wisconsin: the Tundra. And my distaste for the season was only increased because our youngest son Anders was having chronic health issues. Granted he'd always been our sick one, often getting bronchitis which sometimes turned into pneumonia if we didn't get him on antibiotics soon enough. But he was definitely worse during the winter months.

At age four, he was diagnosed with asthma and was regularly using two different inhalers along with Singular- a medication to prevent asthma attacks, every day. But *this* winter, his coughing had us seeking various doctors for reasons as to why he wasn't getting better; only worse. He fell into a cycle of catching a slight cold which would then explode, seemingly overnight, into croup which gave him an awful seal barking type cough. The kind that if we were in public, I received stares that seemed to convey, "What is *wrong* with your kid? Sheesh! Take him home. Or get him to a doctor already."

Sometimes he would develop stridor, a malady which created this high pitched, abnormal, almost musical breathing sound. It was eerie. Fever and wheezing kept Anders up all night and sometimes caused him to cough so hard he would vomit. We'd put him on steroids, antibiotics and cough syrup with codeine. He would recover for about two weeks; I called this his honeymoon period. And then he'd get sick all over again. I was receiving letters from the school warning me that our son was missing too many days. He was absent more than twenty days that year due to illness and doctor appointments. Thankfully, I had a flexible, part-time job employed with a local literacy council so I was able to be available to him and still work from home sometimes. My boss, Jill, was also one of my closest friends and she always allowed me to put family first.

At that time, all of our care was being done at our local clinic and hospital, St. Croix Regional Medical Center. Our primary physician, Dr. Melissa Hall, who also happened to be my best friend, had us see an allergist because there seemed to be more than just asthma plaguing him. The allergist put Anders through a battery of skin testing for possible allergies. Basically, Anders was a human pin cushion. In spite of his young age, he was a model patient and remained still and compliant while being injected in the back and arm with dozens of possible allergens such as pollen, animal dander, dust mites and food. Then, we waited for thirty minutes to see if his little body would react to each one. It was strange to see his skin covered in pricks and dots. I studied them as he lay on the table and the clock ticked. I almost hoped for some sort of a reaction. But in the end, after all of that poking and prodding it turned out Anders was allergic to absolutely nothing. While most parents would think this was good news, I took it as a disappointment because we weren't getting answers. I left feeling frustrated. "Why was my baby always getting sick?" Afterwards, I took Anders for a much deserved Dairy Queen treat. I got one for myself too.

I'd been advised not to go on those analyze yourself, symptom checker websites like WebMD or Diagnose-Me.com. But it drove me nearly insane not knowing. So I ignored the advice and researched anyway. I was given every single possibility of what his symptoms might be related to; from a common cold to pneumothorax, "Say what?" But not being of the medical profession, I would have trouble comprehending the various terms and jargon; especially when I found myself in a medical journal; "What is BURKHOLDERIA CEPACIA COMPLEX or PSEUDOMONAS AERUGINOSA and should this be cause for alarm?" I spent hours on my computer, defining terms. It would sometimes be 10:00 AM and I'd realize I was still in pajamas, in my unmade bed, on my laptop, all crazy-haired and crusty-eyed, causing myself more exhaustion and worry. "Wait, my kid doesn't have a pulmonary embolism does he? What about Bronchial Adenoma?" I should have listened to good advice in the first place and stayed away from the internet!

That said, my research led me to believe that my son might have something more serious than asthma. At our next visit with the allergist, I mustered up the courage to ask him a few questions. I was nervous; after all, I wasn't even close to being a medical professional. I didn't want to sound stupid. And I certainly didn't want to offend this wonderful long time physician whom I respected and was grateful for. But ultimately, my son's well-being was more important than my own personal reputation so I decided to venture and inquire anyway.

"Doctor, when I research Anders' symptoms, I've had things like Cystic Fibrosis come up. Do we need to be concerned about this being a possibility?"

The doctor listened to my words and thought for a moment. "Well, if Anders was born here at our hospital, we can take a look at his history and rule that out right now." He was supportive. Then he went to his computer and did some checking. It took a few minutes but he was able to tell me with confidence,

"According to our hospital records, Anders was screened as a newborn and it looks like he was negative for Cystic Fibrosis." So there; he put an end to *that* worry. What a relief!

From the allergist we were sent to an ear, nose and throat specialist at our local hospital. This doctor performed a laryngoscopy on Anders, sending a flexible scope down the back of his throat. Anders thought it was cool having a camera inside of him and seeing on a monitor what it looked like when he swallowed. I was thankful that his curiosity was stronger than fear. From what the ENT could tell, he suspected reflux and prescribed a medication for it. But after a month, nothing improved. So we tried a second treatment. This too failed and we attempted a third prescription. But Anders' symptoms remained unchanged and he was actually getting worse. Finally, the ENT referred us to a pulmonologist at Children's Hospital in St. Paul, Minnesota. By then we were discouraged, worried and desperate. Hopefully being sent to a specialist at a larger facility would bring us answers.

With all of those doctors and appointments, Anders went through so much poking and prodding, having all kinds of bodily fluids collected, images taken and more, that counting the hours was impossible. It was exhausting for us all but necessary, and I appreciated the thoroughness of his doctors. Anders was always the prize patient. He rarely complained, and I believe there was a small part of him that was even glad to be missing school. I saw that twinkle in his eye when I mentioned he was going to be absent because of another appointment. He was always so good about taking medicine, swallowing pills and even drinking that nasty, chalk-like barium stuff or the terrible tasting prednisolone. He was rarely afraid of needles, tubes or procedures. My other children weren't always so compliant, and I knew how much harder things could have been. I'd experienced with Carson and Ella having to coax, soothe, hold, force, sedate, and even strap them down with tears, screams, and sweat. God was gracious with Anders being so brave. In fact, I believe God was preparing Anders for this path, even before he was born.

When I was pregnant with my children, I felt impressed by the Holy Spirit to pray a specific prayer for each one of them. For Carson, my oldest, it was that he would be wise and make good choices. For Ella, my prayer was for her to be a friend and encouragement to all. And for Anders, my prayer was that he be brave and strong. I prayed these prayers for my children with blind faith, trusting that God knew what He was doing. Now, I was beginning to see it. As they have grown and matured, it is evident in each of their lives how God is answering those prayers in unique and specific ways. With Carson, from a young age, I have seen him show an interest and understanding of God's Word. He asks deep questions about the Bible and shows a desire to learn more about the Lord. With Ella, it is by no coincidence that I have often received comments from parents, coaches, and teachers about her genuine kindness and sincere friendliness to others. She has an exceptional way of encouraging people and making them feel special and included. I know God is using her, and it touches my heart. I am amazed at how our three children are all so unique in spite of growing up in the same house with the same parents and expectations. Thankfully, God created each person with distinctive characteristics. Anders' bravery, stamina, and confidence are evident to all who meet him and I am grateful for that gift.

A memorable example of his outward strength and bravery happened one day at Children's Hospital in St. Paul. We were seeing the pulmonologist who the ENT had recommended to us. It was to be another long day of testing and my kindergarten son insisted that he wear his new Superman costume, complete with cape and built-in pectoral and abdominal muscles. The new Superman movie had just come out and my hero loving boy was absolutely enthralled with it. In fact, I think there was a part of my son that actually believed he *was* Superman. So just before we pulled out of the driveway on our way to the hospital, I gave in to Anders' request to wear his beloved costume and let him run back into the house for it. I told my husband, "With the day we have planned, we need some comic relief!" Anders soon came back into the van with his Superman costume already on. He looked positively radiant with his bleach blond hair and stunning blue eyes against the dark blue suit and bright red cape. I never did see a child more proud to be clothed in such an outfit. He proceeded to wear it the entire day; through the halls, the elevators, the exam rooms, the waiting rooms, the labs, the bathroom, and even the cafeteria. He strutted around with his hands on his hips, ready to save the day at a moment's notice. Everywhere he went he brought a smile- to the patients and their worried caregivers, and to the receptionists, nurses, doctors and other staff. Everyone was accommodating and did very well playing along with Superman.

Anders wore his Superman costume with pride.

During a lab appointment, Anders surprised us all by hopping up onto the table before being asked, pushing up his sleeves and saying in his deepest tough-guy voice, "Go ahead and stab me." His charisma certainly put us at ease about the real reasons we were there. The pulmonologist wanted to investigate a few things, one of them being Cystic Fibrosis- even though Anders' newborn screening had come back negative for this. He assured me that the routine sweat test he ordered, which measures the amount of chloride contained in a person's sweat, was only so we could exclude it completely from our minds. This procedure is the gold-standard in diagnosing CF.

In defense of Anders' allergist who originally told me we could rule out CF, I want to say that this is an extremely complex disease and he was giving us his best educated response. Doctors don't have all of the answers and there is a reason to see specialists. I strongly believe in respectfully asking questions, seeking second opinions, and also in a mother's intuition.

However, those details weren't running through my mind as Anders was put through the thirty-minute procedure. I was too busy marveling at my superhero boy with the bulging pectoral muscles and long red cape. His God-given strength and courage was a saving grace to me and my husband that day. He truly was *our* hero as his bravery kept us distracted and smiling. Although, there was a part of me that thought, "If we can just get through this horrible winter, maybe Anders will turn a corner."

Chapter 2

TICKED OFF

T he test results for the various procedures done at Children's Hospital seemed to take forever and it felt like we were always waiting on something. It nearly drove me insane at the thought of answers about our boy potentially sitting on someone's desk being overlooked. "Maybe they forgot to let me know the results." I kept thinking. My impatience got the best of me so I would call the hospital, sometimes daily. I tried not to and from time to time, I showed self-control. Those times I only called every *other* day. Occasionally I would stare at my phone and telepathically try to get the lab to call me. "Come on lab tech people. You know you want to call me. Ring phone. Ring!"

One of the most difficult scenarios of waiting is when it relates to the well-being of someone you love. What added to our frustration was that when test results finally did begin to trickle in, they offered us no solid answers. We received news such as, "The findings were inconclusive so we need to do further testing." Or, "His numbers were border-line so we'd like to re-administer the procedure." And, "We need to expand our search so it's going to take two more weeks." Ugh! Always more waiting. And more worry.

About the only positive thing happening during this time was the coming of spring. Finally! (Cue the music for: *Vivaldi's Four Season's Spring Concerto*.) The last signs of the dreaded winter had disappeared. Hallelujah! No more icy roads, polar vortex or having to push my grocery cart through a parking lot while having ice pellets assault my cheeks! The snow had melted, leaves were popping, and the grass was slowly turning from dull brown to luscious green; my favorite color. My beloved garden beckoned me. I couldn't wait to help the earth produce colorful flowers, fruits and vegetables. Any free time I had was spent on my knees, getting dirty with a small rake in hand, working the ground and cultivating it. Now, keep in mind, I consider myself a girly-girl. I like make-up and nail polish, cute clothes, and spending time on my hair. But this time of year, I would leave behind all signs of those things. My fingernails took on permanent dirt underneath them and cuts and scratches laced my hands and arms. Forget the gloves- my palms sweat too much. Plus I liked the feel of the plants and dirt. The garden was my happy place. Here, I could forget my troubles for a little while. I could lose track of time, and not realize that it was almost 5:00 PM and my family needed supper shortly. Frozen pizza is okay to have three days in a row, right?

I would soon be reminded that this world has many troubles, even from the places we least expect it. I certainly didn't anticipate my cherished garden to be one of them; where an enemy would come forth and nearly take me down. So tiny, you would need a magnifying glass to identify it. But over the course of a few weeks, it became so big and scary it caused my family and me to fall to our knees and pray.

It began over the first weekend of June. We had a busy few days with out-of-town family visiting; Anders had soccer games, Ella had gymnastics, we took cousins on a trip to the zoo, and then there was to be a birthday party for my husband to finish off the week's festivities. We were going to have twenty-six people over for lunch at our house to celebrate, immediately following church on Sunday. I truly enjoyed having people over and looked forward to the birthday gathering. But I had a nagging headache that made things difficult. This wasn't anything new though. I had dealt with headaches most of my life. I was even being treated by a neurologist for chronic migraines; nearly fifteen of them a month to be exact. But this seemed different because I was also having fevers off and on and some of them were quite high, nearing 103 degrees.

I'm normally a morning person, but on Sunday morning, when the alarm went off, I groaned. At the time, I was probably guilty of being overcommitted, teaching Sunday school, being on worship team and hosting the lunch at my home for twenty-six people all on the same day. That was what my morning looked like. I did not want to get out of bed and I hit snooze. My head still throbbed and a fever and chills made it worse. I asked myself as I reluctantly kicked off the pile of blankets, "How in the world am I going to do all of this?"

Reaching for extra-strength ibuprofen, and my prescription headache medication, I managed to sit up, put one foot in front of the other and get through the busy morning. I taught Sunday school. I helped lead music in church, (although I actually dosed off during the service and it had *nothing* to do with our pastor's sermon). I put on a birthday party for Nathan, feeding over two dozen people in my home. Rachael Ray wouldn't have been impressed, but I did it. As soon as everyone had gone through the food line and appeared to be contentedly filling their stomachs I did something completely uncharacteristic. I went upstairs, grabbed a pillow, a blanket, took a few more meds and went into my back yard near some of my young nephews who were climbing on our playground and lay down in the grass and went to sleep. I slept for two solid hours, right in the middle of my husband's birthday party! What kind of a hostess was I? The next thing I knew, people were waking me up to tell me good bye and what a nice time they had. I was incredibly embarrassed but honestly, I felt too terrible to care. Shortly after everyone left I asked Nathan to take me to the St. Croix Regional Medical Center Emergency Room which was just a few minutes away. "This is the worst headache of my life." I moaned as I clutched an icepack to my forehead. "The pain… it just won't leave me." Nathan put his arm around me and led me to the car.

In the ER, I was given some treatment intravenously and sent home a few hours later. The doctor figured it was just another one of my ongoing migraines. The strong medication helped me sleep some that night but I woke up the next morning with such excruciating pain, I actually dreamed I had been shot in the forehead. I remember pleading for God to just take me home to heaven. Nathan however, was fiercely praying against this as he quickly drove me back to the emergency room. When I reached the hospital, my fever had spiked to 104 causing the doctor to run a complete blood workup on me. When the CBC came back it showed that my white blood cell count was abnormally low, down to 1.3 billion cells. A typical white blood cell count for an adult female would be somewhere between 4.5 and 10 billion cells. My family physician and friend, Melissa, soon arrived to confer with the emergency room doctor and the decision was made to admit me. Nathan didn't like the direction this was going, but when it was determined I was staying, I felt relief. Call it intuition, I sensed this was more than just a migraine headache and after all of the back and forth we'd been doing, it felt reassuring that the hospital was going to try and get to the bottom of my illness and hopefully give us some answers. It seemed like we were always looking for answers.

Once I was wheeled into a patient room and given comforts like pillows and privacy, I was able to relax in spite of the hideously revealing hospital gown. I would be sure to have Nathan bring me some of my favorite pajamas from home as soon as possible. The medications I had been given were finally taking the edge off of my pain and now I was able to notice the toll this experience was having on my poor husband. I could see the anxiety etched in his face and I wanted more than anything to ease his worry. So I decided to use my sense of humor and think of some positives for being at the hospital. Maybe it was the pain killers talking, but when I got to thinking; I found all kinds of reasons that hospitals were a fabulous place to be. I shared them with Nathan in a comedy of lists.

First, the crushed ice. They use a machine that makes it almost like snow cone consistency. Grape juice poured over it helped me with nausea. And as I burned with fever, it was a cool, refreshing treat. Forget the baseball park, just head to your local hospital for a flavored snow cone treat!

Second, I relished the heated blankets the nurses tucked in around me whenever I requested. To me, they felt like the most calming warm hug, especially when a high fever made me ache all over or feel deliriously cold and shivering. What a comfort! Who needed a massage therapist? A warm heated blanket would do the trick.

Third, the nurse call button. "Yes, could I get another lime Popsicle and some more crushed ice in my water bottle please? Oh and my pillow needs fluffing." If I wasn't feeling so terribly ill I might have actually enjoyed my hospital stay. Just add a pool and hot tub and we were practically at the Holiday Inn! Okay I'm exaggerating. Most would agree the smells in hospitals versus hotels are on the opposite spectrum.

Nathan and I had a good laugh. But we were on a roller coaster. I was exhausted but felt there was little time to truly rest as the experts tried to rule out various diseases, complications and ultimately figure out what was going on inside my body. I was given morphine for the pain and a CT scan of my brain. Results were inconclusive and more tests were ordered. My pain meds were later increased to dilaudid and I required oxygen. Nathan went home to be with the kids that first night in hopes of keeping some sense of normalcy. But in the morning, I continued to decline. On day two of my hospital stay, I was told by my neurologist that I needed to have a spinal tap to completely rule out meningitis. I pictured a gigantic foot-long needle piercing my spine as it sucked out a liter or more of necessary fluid. The thought of this, although completely exaggerated from the actual procedure, brought terrible fear! But there was more. The specialist was concerned that my white blood cell count was too low. So before the spinal tap, I would first need a platelet transfusion to help my body prepare and become strong enough to handle the procedure. No amount of heated blankets or ice chips could calm me at this point. I was a wreck! After the doctor left, I tried calling Nathan to fill him in on this latest information but he didn't answer his phone. I tried contacting my mom but she didn't answer either. I suddenly felt so alone and frightened! Finally, I prayed that God would send someone to comfort me.

"Please God! I'm so scared! I know you're with me but I need something or someone tangible right now." And maybe ten seconds later, I heard a knock. "Come in?" I said tentatively. The door slowly opened and in walked my pastor, Dave Williams and his wife Sheri, coming to visit me! I thanked the Lord and with tears and a relieved smile I told my visitors that they were an absolute and immediate answer to my prayer. A few hours later, with Nathan devotedly by my side, I went through the spinal tap with flying colors. I even asked to take a selfie with the gigantic needle but Nathan surprisingly wouldn't let me. Later I realized he was actually doing me a favor because of how sick and hideous I probably looked. No one needed to have that image lodged in their brain, I certainly didn't.

That evening Nathan brought the kids to see me. I was beginning to get homesick and missed them terribly. Nathan tried to seem casual during the visit, as if everything was routine and mom was just here because of a bad headache. But when I saw the looks on my children's faces, I knew they weren't buying it. Ella tentatively approached my bed and then carefully reached out to trace the IVs and oxygen tubing. She whispered a few questions and then buried her head into me and started to cry. Anders wanted to immediately snuggle in bed with me. Carson just stood back with a white face, afraid to touch me. They didn't stay too long. It was a school night and Nathan needed to get them home and ready for bed. This was going to be hard on everyone and we didn't know how long it would last.

My hospital stay continued and I began to develop some strange symptoms including involuntary tremors in my body. Muscles in my legs, arms and shoulders would spasm, day and night. It was kind of funny but also unsettling. What in the world was wrong with me? Also, around the fourth day being hospitalized I began experiencing heaviness in my chest. It felt as if someone was pressing on my left side. I asked the nurses to turn up my oxygen but when that didn't help I started to panic.

"What's happening to me? Why does it feel so hard to breathe?" I thought, though I didn't say this out loud. Nathan already looked white as a ghost. The on-call doctor ordered an EKG and then a CT scan of my lungs and the unexpected results were a very peculiar case of pneumonia. Little spots infiltrated evenly all throughout my left lung. It was so strange! The Department of Infectious Diseases at Mayo Clinic was even consulted and I was put on three aggressive antibiotics to combat whatever this strange compilation of illnesses was.

During that difficult time however, I was given several things that gave me peace and assurance. The first was a Bible verse.

> 2 Corinthians 12:9 NIV, *"But He said to me, 'My grace is sufficient for you, for my power is made perfect in weakness.' Therefore I will boast all the more gladly about my weaknesses, so that Christ's power may rest on me."*

I had never felt so weak in my entire life. But it was encouraging to know God could actually use me in my current state to show His power. When I was weak, that's when His strength could be revealed and made complete. I also realized, the only thing that was important- and I mean truly essential in life was receiving God's grace. It was all I needed. No amount of material possessions, luxuries, or even test results- whether it be mine or Anders, came close. Only His grace sufficed. And with that in mind, I rested with complete peace.

A few days later, we were *finally* given the breakthrough we had been waiting for. Melissa was checking up on me one afternoon and I happened to mention that my back was irritating me. I had a burning sensation and it felt hot to the touch. She decided to lift up my gown and do an examination. It soon became very clear what we were dealing with.

"Oh… Oh wow!" She said with some surprise in her voice.

"What!? What is it?" I wasn't expecting that kind of reaction and it made me very curious. She called my husband over and they began talking behind my back; literally.

"Hey! That's not fair! You guys need to tell me what's going on! I'm the patient here. What do you see?" I demanded.

Melissa explained, "Erythema migrans- it's an expanding rash, or commonly called a bulls-eye rash. And you've got a big one Leanne, about a foot in diameter across the middle of your back!"

We all had a sort of 'ah-ha' moment as she continued, "Well, this makes *a lot* of sense now…"The bulls-eye rash she found was a characteristic sign for Lyme disease which is caused by the bite of a deer tick infected with the Borrelia bacterium. And where we live in Western Wisconsin, we have one of the highest concentrations for Lyme disease in the entire nation. I felt fortunate because not everyone with Lyme will get the target shaped rash. It was bad but at least I knew!

After several more days in the hospital it was determined I had not one but two aggressive tick-borne diseases, probably from the very same deer tick: Lyme and Ehrlichiosis. It was hard to believe that a tiny parasite could wreak such havoc in a person's life. I thought I was ready to meet Jesus! My family was grateful it wasn't my time yet, and so was I.

During that period, God continued to use His people to show love to me and my family. Visitors came. Flowers, treats, gift cards, and meals were given and it was encouraging and humbling. People even came and cleaned my house and folded my laundry. I have to admit this wasn't easy for me. Even though I was extremely exhausted having just spent a week in the hospital, I had a difficult time giving up control of my household. It felt uncomfortable allowing my friends and family to scrub my toilets or vacuum for me. But I remember hearing someone once say, "Don't take away my opportunity to bless you." Humbly, I knew exactly what she meant. It feels really good knowing you've encouraged someone by taking them a meal or helping with a project. But everyone's incredible generosity completely overwhelmed me at times and I thought, "How do we ever thank these people enough?" After pondering it for a while, Nathan and I realized our friends and family wouldn't have wanted us to repay them for their kind gestures; because that wasn't the point. I came across scripture that spoke very uniquely to this situation.

> Hebrews 6:10, *"God is not unjust; He will not forget your work and the love you have shown Him as you have helped His people and continue to help them."*

God saw our friends' good deeds and it pleased Him. What a wonderful realization for them to know they were making God happy. I made sure to share this verse with those who were blessing us. I also realized through the humble position I found myself in, combined with the acts of kindness from others, God can show us in specific and tender ways that we are valued and cared for. We certainly felt much love during that period in our lives.

After a week of being hospitalized I was finally discharged! That crushed ice machine just wasn't enough to make me want to stay any longer. I actually begged my doctors to let me go home, assuring them I would be diligent about taking it easy and continuing my treatments orally. Tick-borne diseases can sometimes have long term effects on a person leaving them with chronic pain, neurological suffering, and more. But it was hopeful that my case was detected early and doctors thought I would fully recover after another month of aggressive antibiotics and rest.

I was left utterly and completely exhausted. Honestly, I had this fantasy that once I returned home, l would be able to slip back into my normal routine and most importantly, spend time with my kids. As a sentimentalist, I felt really disappointed that I had missed out on their entire last week of school. I didn't get to see Anders' Kindergarten music concert, or volunteer at the end-of-the-year Sports Day like I usually do. I missed a field trip and didn't get to say good-bye to their teachers on the last day of school. But now it was summer vacation and I tried to counter the mom-guilt I carried by thinking of fun things I could do with my children. Go to the park, take bike rides, and hit the beach. Except for one problem- I was completely zapped of strength, barely able to walk up our simple flight of stairs. Where was that nurse call button when I needed it?

As I adjusted to my first day back home, the kids headed out to play without me. I sat down at the kitchen table alone and stared at the flowers and cards which graced our counters. We had a freezer and fridge full of meals for the next several weeks. I knew I had a lot to be grateful for. But irrational guilt and sadness tugged at my heart and I battled gloomy feelings.

Suddenly, I was jerked to attention when the phone rang. I looked down at the caller ID. It was the Pulmonologist's office from Children's Hospital. We had put on hold all of our worries about Anders with me being hospitalized. Now, here was the phone call we had been waiting for; hopefully the call with answers. And yet… did I really want to know, right now? Was I strong enough to handle it? Home alone?

> Isaiah 41:10, "*So do not fear, for I am with you; do not be dismayed, for I am your God. I will strengthen you and help you; I will uphold you with my righteous right hand.*"

Chapter 8

HE'LL HELP YOU CATCH
YOUR BREATH

I did my best to keep my voice calm and hold back the adrenaline rush I felt as I answered my phone. A kind woman was on the other line.

"Hi Mrs. Waterworth, this is the nurse from pulmonology. Is this a good time for you?"

For a split second I thought about saying "no" and then going into a long account of my recent tick disease perils. But my better judgement kicked in and I lied, saying it was the perfect time to talk. The nurse on the other line continued.

"I want to discuss Anders' results with you. It looks like everything we tested him for came back normal... except for the sweat test."

I had done some research so I wouldn't be completely in the dark regarding this procedure and its findings. I knew the sweat test measured the amount of chloride contained in a person's sweat. I mentally ticked off the levels and what they meant.

(Note: mmol/L = millimole per Liter)

A Chloride level of:

39 mmol/L or less= Cystic Fibrosis is very unlikely

40 – 59 mmol/L = borderline means that Cystic Fibrosis is possible

60 mmol/L or greater = Cystic Fibrosis is present.

I took a deep breath, cringed, and said, "Okay. So there's good news and bad news?"

The nurse continued, "His numbers were kind of unusual and we'd like to have him come in for some blood work at our genetic counseling office. Then, we will hopefully get a better idea of what exactly we are dealing with." As we discussed appointment dates and where the clinic was located, I jotted a few things down and tried to remain in control. I cautiously asked,

"I know you can't tell me very much right now but will you at least share what his sweat test numbers were?"

The nurse hesitated and then told me, "We always run the test twice. And it looks like Anders numbers were a 58/59… But I don't want this to alarm you."

I believe it was at that very moment my motherly instinct told me my son had Cystic Fibrosis. The nurse didn't want to scare me. But her words were like a sucker punch in the stomach because I knew that 60 meant a positive diagnosis for the disease. Anders' numbers were nearly there. How could he NOT have it? The nurse tried to assure me that these results did not necessarily mean Cystic Fibrosis was certain. But at that point I wanted to get off the phone as fast as possible. I knew Anders had CF.

Once the conversation finally ended, I was panic stricken and felt like I had the wind knocked out of me. I began to hyperventilate, shake and sob, the tears pouring down my cheeks. My worst nightmare was coming true.

When Anders was told to have this particular test done, I had my homework done. I understood what these numbers meant. Web MD told me that Cystic Fibrosis was a genetic, life threatening illness with no known cure. At that time, the average life expectancy was thirty-seven years of age. I was currently thirty-six. I didn't feel old. I figured I had my whole life ahead of me. And I did! But did Anders?

The tears wouldn't stop now. My shoulders shook hard and I put my face in my hands weeping desperately. I could handle an illness if it was mine. But this was different. This was my son. My baby!

It was my job to protect Anders and make sure he stayed healthy. With this news, I didn't know if I could. I was home alone and all I wanted was someone to wrap their arms around me, hold me tight, and tell me it was just a bad dream. I cried like a child as I sat by myself at the kitchen table, weeping so hard I struggled to inhale and exhale much like I did in the hospital with pneumonia, except this pain was worse, and no antibiotics would help.

How was I going to tell my husband this news? And our children? How do you explain to your own son he might have a disease that would keep him from living into adulthood? I just didn't know how I could ever do any of this. I couldn't! The weight of it all was crushing. I was terrified! I was angry! It felt heavy and pressing and nearly took my breath away.

And then, in between sobs, I heard the ticking of the clock on our fireplace mantle. I exhaled and listened to it for a moment as it brought me back to the present. Tick-tock, tick-tock, tick-tock… In spite of a seemingly out of control life, time kept moving forward. Was it possible I could too?

In that moment, God saw me. I wasn't alone. He knew my pain. After all, His Son suffered too- and even died. God understood how I felt. And He was there with me. I breathed in a slow life-giving breath and closed my eyes, folded my arms on the table and rested my weary head. I knew I could keep moving forward.

> Psalm 34:18 MSG, *"If your heart is broken, you'll find God right there; if you're kicked in the gut He'll help you catch your breath."*

~Understanding Cystic Fibrosis~

I want to take a moment and give some background information on Cystic Fibrosis. I recognize that many are unfamiliar with this disease. I spent a great deal of research and even had to teach my children how to say its name properly as it is difficult to pronounce. They had to practice saying it slow at first; *Sis-tik Fi-bro-sis.*

There is a cute story which has been circulating for decades about a little boy with Cystic Fibrosis. One day he heard his mother talking on the phone about his disease. When this young boy overheard her say the words "Cystic Fibrosis", he thought she was saying "sixty-five roses". The mother was touched by her son's mistake because he saw something beautiful in a disease that can often be quite ugly. The phrase "sixty-five roses" is now a registered trademark of the Cystic Fibrosis Foundation, which adopted the rose as its symbol.

But the easiest way to say and remember it is by simply calling it CF. Sadly though; there is nothing simple about it. CF is a complicated and rare disease, affecting only about 30,000 people in the United States, and 70,000 worldwide; most commonly among Caucasians. During the early 1990's when I was a young teen, I first learned of CF because a family in our church had a daughter with the disease who was around six or seven years old. I babysat for this family once in a while and witnessed this beautiful little girl doing her percussive therapy which was supposed to help loosen mucus from her lungs. Back then, I was told that her life expectancy was only about twenty-one years of age. That startled me. Around that same time, I learned that two distant maternal second cousins of mine also had CF and one of them recently succumbed to the illness. They were siblings- a brother and a sister, and it was the sister who had passed away. From what I had heard about CF, my cousin's lungs had filled up with mucus in the end and she died a miserable early death in her twenties. It sounded horrifying. That's about all I knew of it.

CF is an inherited, genetic disease that people are born with.

Sometimes, parents don't even realize it runs in their family. It can go undetected for years skipping generations and then suddenly appear, seemingly from out of nowhere.

Typically, people with CF are diagnosed before the age of two. This is either because symptoms present themselves early or the newborn screening detects a diagnosis. But in order for CF to happen, both mom and dad need to be carriers of a mutated CFTR gene. This defective gene makes a protein that controls the movement of salt and water in and out of your body's cells- and it doesn't work very well. It causes thick, sticky mucus and very salty sweat. This is why the sweat test is considered the gold standard in diagnosing CF. The disease wouldn't be officially discovered until 1938 but references dating back as far as 1595 indicate that people understood some of its unique characteristics. A chilling old Irish saying went like this,

"If your baby tastes of salt, he is not long for this world."

And a widely used quotation from a Swiss Almanac of children's songs and games dating back to 1857 says,

"The child will soon die whose brow tastes salty when kissed".

These indicate that a salty taste on the skin of a child gave him a poor prognosis. People didn't realize it at the time, but they were talking about Cystic Fibrosis.

The main source of problems among CF patients is the thick sticky mucus which infiltrates the organs such as the lungs and digestive system. Common symptoms are persistent coughing, wheezing, sinus infections, frequent lung infections, obstruction of the pancreas and the body's ability to break down the absorption of food, and malnourishment. Fifty years ago, if your baby was diagnosed with CF, he or she wouldn't live long enough to go to kindergarten. But today, with modern medicine and innovative therapies, nearly 50% of the CF population is age eighteen or older and as of 2017, the average life expectancy is approximately forty years.

I guess I should feel good about this but I don't because that's how old I am. And frankly, I don't feel that old. Some people joke that forty is over the hill. But it's really not. A forty-year-old still has a majority of their life ahead of them. And to live this long, someone with CF must be extremely diligent and hard working. CF patients must take dozens of medications every single day for the rest of their lives with the hope that it will keep them healthy such as enzymes, antibiotics, inhalers, vitamins, supplements, steroids, sinus rinses, allergy, asthma, and reflux medications, along with nebulized treatments and other unique therapies.

One of the newer technologies used in treating CF is something called the airway clearance system, or the Vest. Because the thick sticky mucus can clog organs such as the lungs, it's important to keep them clear. One way to do so is by literally pounding or clapping on them! Years ago, people would have the CF patient lay down on a table or bed angled downward and then pound or clap on their back and chest and allow the child to cough up mucus. As you can imagine, this was time-consuming and uncomfortable for everyone involved- unless you were the older brother or sister and had a little bit of a vendetta against your sibling. In some cases, this manual clapping therapy is still used.

Thankfully, within the last three decades, a wonderful team of doctors and scientists from the University of Minnesota have invented a genius piece of medical equipment called the Vest. Patients actually wear a type of clothing article like a vest. It is fitted perfectly to the size of each patient and stays on with snaps, Velcro and buckles. There are tubes that attach to the Vest and then to an air compressor. The machine is plugged in and programmed specifically to the needs of each patient. Then, the Vest fills up with air with great force and vibrates; the Vest actually does the job of pounding the lungs thousands of times per minute, but with perfect efficiency, speed, and calculated pressure, keeping the airways more open and free from the thick, constricting mucus. It's loud and it shakes, making the person's voice sound like they're in a helicopter. Vesting is done in conjunction with a nebulizer which turns liquid medication into a mist. When inhaled into the lungs, the vapors can help thin out mucus and open up the airways. Typically, a patient will do Vest therapy for thirty minutes in the morning and thirty minutes at night. And when they are experiencing illness, they add sessions. But these minutes literally add years to their life. When this machine was first invented, the compressor was about the size of a large refrigerator. Today, it is similar to that of the smallest microwave.

As of most recent, there is now a "miracle" drug which has come down the pipeline called Orkambi. It is the first drug of its kind directed at treating the *cause* of the disease. The FDA has approved the use of Orkambi in children with CF as young as age six who have two copies of the most common CF mutation, named the F508del. Of the 30,000 people in the United States with CF, approximately 11,000 will be positively affected by this. It is an optimistic step in the right direction and other drugs are soon to follow that will apply to other mutations.

A last resort option for CF patients which developed within the last thirty-five years is the miracle of lung transplantation. While this doesn't cure a person's CF, it does give them a second chance at breathing with new healthy lungs and adding years to their time on earth.

They truly have made great strides in extending the life of those with CF. If ever there was a good time for a child to be diagnosed with this disease, it's now. But truth be told, it's still a very frightening, multifaceted, and cruel disease. CF is progressive and there is no known cure.

We didn't know anything for certain about Anders, but things were feeling more and more likely that this could be his diagnosis and our future.

Chapter 4

LAYING IT DOWN

"Yes, I'm feeling much better, thank you Mary. Yes, of course I still plan on being the Vacation Bible School emcee and song leader. Don't worry! I'll learn all ten of the new songs along with the choreography... And yes, I'll get my lines memorized for the skits. Sure I can gather up the necessary props too. No problem... Yes, I'm very excited!"

I believe God has a sense of humor which is good because so do I. And He knows that I'm a "yes-girl" and I get excited about an opportunity- which also means I can be guilty of overcommitting. So while I was supposed to be resting and taking it easy after being in the hospital, I was also on the phone with our church worship director, putting her mind at ease. At that time, we attended Hope Evangelical Free Church in Osceola, Wisconsin, which was about eight miles from our home.

I *was* excited. My extroverted personality loved being on stage, singing, acting silly and praising Jesus with about one hundred adorable little kids! But seriously, what was I doing to myself? Was this really what God had in mind? My husband and doctor weren't so sure. But in the end, I thought it might be a good distraction. Because resting on the couch only caused me to worry about Anders and feel sorry for myself. So during the end of June, I began sorting through Vacation Bible School materials. And in God's providential way, he spoke to me in the most personal manner.

For the event, the children's ministry team chose to do a medieval theme called Kingdom Rock and our focus was all about standing strong through the trials of life. I ended up having to learn and memorize songs titled, *Don't Worry Just Pray, Stand Strong When Life Changes,* and *Pray About Everything.*

Literally, when I'd be feeling overwhelmed or scared about the unknown with Anders, I'd have to listen to a song with lyrics that told me,

"Don't worry about anything- Just pray about everything!"

"Ha ha!" I thought. "Very funny, God! Okay, I get the message, loud and clear!"

Once, when I was feeling extremely nauseous from some of the medications I was still taking after my illness, a VBS song came to my rescue just when I needed it, *"Stand strong through the ups and downs! Stand Strong for you know that God is in control!"* Every single time I listened to that Vacation Bible School CD I found myself in a puddle of tears and yet completely encouraged. My kids would see me and say,

"Oh great, she's crying again." I would start to laugh and answer, "No guys, Mom's just got allergies!" But truly, God was teaching me so much about trust and dependence on Him through those children's songs. It was hard not to feel His love and presence.

During that time, Anders, Nathan and I needed to meet with a genetic counselor at Children's Hospital in St. Paul. Our first appointment with her was a long one. We spent over an hour discussing family history, answering and asking questions, and trying to understand the complicated nature of CF. We learned more about how far reaching it is. Not only does CF affect the lungs and digestive tract but it also tangles with the reproductive system causing 98% of males who have the disease to be infertile. This news took our breath away.

"Please, God no," I thought. "Are you telling me my son won't get to be a father someday?" This was just one more reason to make this incurable disease an absolutely wretched one. I hated CF.

Anders also had to give a blood sample at the lab. The genetic counselor reminded us that his sweat test numbers showed that it was likely but not absolutely positive that he had CF. So now we were going to look at his genes and search specifically for CF mutations.

Today, researchers have identified approximately 1,800 gene mutations that can cause CF. But in order for CF to be passed on, the mutations need to come from both parents. Anders would need to receive one mutation from me and one from Nathan. I made sure our counselor knew that CF did run in my maternal side of the family. After doing some research, I was able to track down the names of the mutations from those distant family members and give that information to the lab so they could check for those first. She was glad to hear that Nathan's side had no known record of CF in his family but communicated to us that it was still possible to find something because CF is known to skip generations. The plan was for the lab to study Anders' genes, looking for the most common 1,000 mutations, and see if anything came up. If nothing did, they would do a second search looking for the more rare 800 plus mutations and then go from there. But I told myself, "one step at a time." We were told this would take about seven days. In the meantime, I had some dance moves and song lyrics to rehearse like, "*Don't worry about anything. Just pray about everything!*" I would try my very best to do just that.

Kingdom Rock VBS was fast approaching and my strength was slowly gaining. We were all getting excited as the church stage was transformed into a castle and my best Elizabethan accent was practiced as often as possible. I was also glued to my phone in case the hospital called. There were about thirty-five adults and teens on the VBS leadership team and they all knew I was waiting on results about Anders. I felt incredibly supported by them in prayer and love so there was no place I'd rather be. During our opening day with about one hundred cheering, joyful faces, we praised God for His faithfulness in the midst of trials and fears.

When the phone call from our genetic counselor finally did come, I was at home making supper. I left my preparations and the noise of my children and went out onto the patio, shutting the glass door behind me. Again, there was good news and bad.

"We ran the most common mutations and didn't find anything, including the ones that run in your family Leanne." I was thrilled with that news! But my excitement dissipated with her next statement.

"Now, we move into the next phase which is a more advanced search. We'll look through the uncommon CF mutations and see if anything shows up. Unfortunately this will take a little longer so you will need to give us another one to two weeks for results." Without meaning to, I gave a very heavy sigh.

"I'm so sorry, Leanne. I'm sure this has been a really difficult process for your family. I will call you as soon as I get results, okay?" The geneticist was filled with compassion as she spoke. And really, every single medical professional we'd ever dealt with in the last six months was wonderful to work with. But I was just so tired of constantly waiting, waiting, and more waiting. Waiting can be excruciatingly hard! But God gently reminded me to be patient.

Psalm 27:14 NIV, *"Wait for the Lord; be strong and take heart and wait for the Lord."*

Day three of Kingdom Rock arrived and the theme for that day was, "Don't worry. Instead pray!" My script as emcee called for me to perform a skit during the final large-group session of the day. My character was supposed to amble around the sanctuary hauling a ridiculous amount of suitcases and backpacks while having an audible conversation with the Lord. Our pastor played the voice of God and he hid behind the sound booth with a microphone. The skit opened with me struggling to carry my heavy burdens.

"Leanne, I see you've got quite a load there! Would you like some help with those things? I'd be glad to carry them for you." God said to me graciously.

"Oh, no thanks, Lord; I've got this. I'm super strong. I work-out, you know." I replied proudly as I struggled to hold it all together. The kids giggled as I huffed and puffed.

"But Leanne, I'm absolutely willing to take your burdens for you if you will just lay them down at my feet."

"Oh Lord," I said with a chuckle. "I really appreciate your offer, but I'll be fine! I actually *like* hanging on to all of this baggage myself. I got this... No problem. (Stopping to give a thumbs-up) Thanks anyway God!"

(I really hammed it up, struggling and dropping a bag or two, breathing heavily, and staggering as I made my way to the front of the stage.)

My character went back and forth with the Lord a little more and then finally, I crumbled under the pressure and weight of my burdens realizing my need for a Savior. One of the suitcases fell from underneath my arm.

"Please help me Lord! I'm so tired and I can't do this alone." I cried out.

Our medieval set was complete with a regal throne. I cautiously and reluctantly approached it, humbly laying down my suitcases and backpacks, bowing low at the foot of it as if God Himself was seated there. And even though I realized I was only acting, to some part of me it was incredibly real.

The suitcases I carried represented my worries and fears for Anders' health, because I wanted control of it all and clung tightly, not wanting to let go. I was his mother after all. It was my job to take care of him and fix things. But I knew I had to release those thoughts. I didn't want to! But I had to. As I moved toward the stage, with my variety of suitcases and backpacks, I visualized placing my little blond boy at the feet of Jesus. With him I laid down his health, my plans and my dreams for him. I laid it all down. I thought about

Abraham laying down his precious son, Isaac on the altar. Anders was God's child and God knew best. He cared even more for Anders than I ever could.

At that moment I understood and accepted that my son's medical condition was totally out of my hands. I had zero control over the genetic test results we were currently waiting for. I don't think the audience noticed the tears stinging my eyes as our skit came to a close. Anders certainly didn't. I caught a glimpse of him with his buddies in the second row. He was smiling, holding up a craft he had made that morning and completely oblivious to the worry I had just released. I asked the children to stand and we ended our time by reciting the daily Bible verse.

1 Peter 5:7, *"Cast all your cares upon Him for He cares for you."*

Then we lifted our voices together and sang out a worship song that I had taught them called, *"We Fall Down."* The lyrics were like a prayer from my heart.

"We fall down
We lay our crowns
At the feet of Jesus
The greatness of
Your mercy and love
At the feet of Jesus".

Visualizing Anders on the altar gave me a tiny peek through a window of what God did with His one and only Son Jesus. God loved His Son too and yet was willing to sacrifice Him for our sake, because he also loved His people.

> John 3:16, *"For God so loved the world that He gave his one and only Son, that whoever believes in Him, shall not perish but have eternal life."*

Jesus could have said no to God's plan, but instead, he said in submission, "Not my will but yours be done." From there, he willingly suffered on a cross to pay the penalty for our sins so that we could someday spend eternity in heaven. This was God's plan to save us. And this was the hope *our* family relied upon when the fear of a life-threatening disease came crashing down. Yes, we would still feel scared or worried sometimes. These are normal, human emotions. And when these thoughts arise, God instructs us to cast our worries on Him because He cares for us. I will admit, this is not something that comes naturally for me. I need reminders; I am not in control. But God makes a much better driver than I do. He's got the map! And when I am able to surrender, to His will, and His plan, I find myself at peace. I'm grateful that we have a personal and loving God to rely upon when times get tough.

There were mixed feelings for all of us when the week of Vacation Bible School came to a close. The kids had such a blast and I would miss the hugs and smiles from my young audience. The children energized me with their enthusiasm over the songs, dancing, and Bible lessons each day. But the work to keep the momentum going throughout the week took its toll, and by the end, I was pretty wiped out. However, as kids and adults learned about God's promises and to hide His Word in their heart, those eternal rewards were well worth the efforts. For me personally, it helped to break up the anxiety of constantly waiting on those stressful phone calls from the hospital with hopeful test results. For months, it felt like that's all I ever did. I waited!

Just a few days after VBS ended, we received yet another call from the genetics office. I braced myself, fearing the worst possible news as the counselor spoke.

"It appears that in our expanded search for CFTR genes, the test results showed that Anders does indeed have two mutations." I stopped breathing, but kept listening as she continued.

"However, the results are inconclusive. The first variant is what we call *a 5T poly T* tract and the other is a variant of *uncertain significance*. We've never seen it before. But it does have a name. It's called N396D. Other than that, we don't know much about this variant at all. In other words, we don't know whether or not it actually causes CF." I tried really hard to wrap my brain around everything she was saying to me.

"We'd like to do blood work on you and your husband to know which one of you passed these mutations on to Anders. In order for your son to have CF, one mutation needs to come from mom and one from dad. So basically, what it comes down to is this; let's say Leanne, that you carry both of these mutations. Then that would mean Anders does not have CF. But if you carry the 5T poly T tract and Nathan carries the N396D, then that would indicate Anders does have CF. Does this help you understand it better?"

Ugh. My head hurt. CF was so complicated! Why didn't I decide to be a biologist or a chemist when I grew up? Oh yes, that's right... because science was my least favorite subject in school! I knew that when I chose to become a parent, I also agreed to be a nurse, cook, teacher, judge, parole officer, cleaning lady, chauffer, gymnastics and soccer coach. But now a geneticist? Sheesh!

As she spoke, I took notes and repeated things back to make sure I understood and had written them down correctly. When our conversation ended I immediately called Melissa. She was such a blessing to us not only as our family physician but as an understanding friend.

Recently, Melissa's two nieces from Nebraska were diagnosed with Cystic Fibrosis, so she was quite knowledgeable in this area. I quickly told her everything that the genetic counselor had just explained.

Within minutes, Melissa had arranged for me and Nathan to give a blood sample at our local clinic. They would have it sent off to the appropriate test center as soon as possible. Now, we wouldn't have to make the fifty minute drive down to the Children's Hospital and we could have results that much sooner. But it still meant more waiting. As usual. Nathan and I requested that our church body pray for us through an email prayer-chain. We also asked the elders to pray over Anders. Through this, we felt some of the burden lift from our shoulders and trusted that God was in control.

Philippians 4:6-7 *"Do not be anxious about anything, but in every situation, by prayer and petition, with thanksgiving, present your requests to God. And the peace of God, which transcends all understanding, will guard your hearts and your minds in Christ Jesus."*

During that following week, our minds were distracted by a terrible tragedy unfolding in our rural community. Before I went to bed one evening in July, I saw a Facebook post from a friend. Apparently his neighbor's two-year-old boy, Isaiah, was missing and he was asking people to come out and help in the search. A sickening feeling came over me. I couldn't imagine what that would be like to have your child just vanish. It was after 10:00 PM. What if that was my baby lost out there? How terrifying! I also learned that this family had attended our church's Vacation Bible School the week before. Nathan and I immediately went to God in prayer for this local family.

In the morning, I discovered that the boy still hadn't been found. I felt compelled to help look for him. I got a babysitter for my kids, and drove to the search area, about eight miles from our house. As I neared the scene, my heart sank as I realized this was something bigger than expected.

Emergency vehicles were everywhere, and traffic was heavy on a normally quiet stretch of highway. Deputies directed the volunteer searchers to park and check in at a local business. From there, I was given a water bottle, told to register, and then I waited for instructions from police. It was only 9:30 AM and already the weather was becoming unbearably hot and humid. Expected highs for the day were near ninety degrees. Hundreds of volunteers turned out for the search and rescue and it was a somber mood as I began to recognize some friends and other folks from our community who also came out to help. I was put into a team that was taken by bus about a mile from the family's home. As we drove further and further away I kept thinking, "Could a two-year-old child really wander this far from home?" Once the bus stopped, we were told to form a line and trudge through an area of corn fields and thick woods. I begged God to help this innocent little blond haired, blue-eyed boy so he would be found alive soon. My heart ached, especially for his mama. I couldn't imagine the anguish she was going through. I did *a lot* of praying that day. I thought of my own little boy too. And even though I worried for Anders, the realization that someone else's son was in immediate and life threatening danger made me put this family's needs ahead of my own. I continued in the search for the remainder of the day. Hours went by and finally, the humid, emotional hike took its toll. I realized it was time to call it a day.

Then suddenly, in the middle of a field, with spotty cell phone coverage, my phone sprang to life with an incoming call. I looked at the caller ID and it was the geneticist with the final results we'd been waiting for. I quickly moved out of position from our search line, my legs taking wide steps over corn stalks to answer the call. I was a bit out of breath and the counselor asked if it was an okay time for me. I looked around me considering my sad circumstances and briefly explained the situation that I was in. But I reassured her that I had been waiting expectantly for her call and I was ready to listen.

She began to communicate in gentle, comforting tones and I knew, before she told me. Our son had CF. It was finally confirmed. The news was hard to swallow even though I had mentally prepared myself for the worst. She continued, but I was only half listening. Something about Anders needing to be seen by the director of the Cystic Fibrosis Clinic for immediate examination. I was distracted; the hot sun was beating down on me, dogs were barking and people were calling out for Isaiah. The counselor brought me back with, "I'm so sorry Leanne."

It was tough news, but the timing gave me such deep perspective. As I gazed out across the field and watched a line of my fellow search and rescue team members, I knew I still had a reason to be thankful. At the end of the day, I had three children at home waiting for me and I looked forward to giving them the biggest hug ever. Not far from where I stood, there was a mama who didn't know where her baby was or if she'd ever get to see him again. When I ended the call, I knew I still had a job to do. Finish out my search for a missing two-year-old boy.

Sadly, just hours later, we learned on the evening news that the body of Isaiah Theiss was discovered in the trunk of a car on his family's property. It was a tragic and horrific accident. Yes, I had much to be grateful for. That night, I held all of my children close and tight, thanking God for each one of them.

> Revelation 21:4, *"He will wipe away every tear from their eyes, and death shall be no more, neither shall there be mourning, nor crying, nor pain anymore, for the former things have passed away."*

Chapter 5

It Is Well With My Soul

A few years back, in the fall of 2006, before I knew about Anders' CF, I attended a Hearts at Home conference. This is an annual weekend event for Christian moms in Rochester, Minnesota. It was a chance for me to take a short break away from the kids, have fun with my girlfriends, and gain wisdom on parenting and marriage. I looked forward to it every year. During that weekend, something that really made an impression on me was a concept our keynote speaker, Jennifer Rothschild shared. Rothschild is a wife and mother who also happened to be blind. As she spoke to the audience of 2,000 women, her words stunned me. She said, "Even if it is not well with your circumstances, it can still be well with your soul." What a compelling statement and testimony coming from someone who lived in complete darkness. She continued, "You can still have joy in spite of whatever trials you are experiencing in your life." She closed out her powerful message by leading us in the familiar hymn; *It is Well with my Soul.* I shut my eyes and took in the sound of 2,000 voices singing together.

At that time, I didn't have any difficulties to complain about. Remember, this was before Lyme, Ehrlichiosis, and CF. Things were going pretty smoothly as Nathan and I raised our young, seemingly healthy children. I was content as a stay-at-home-mom, expecting our third child while Nathan was employed at his dream job and we lived in a beautiful, newly built home. I figured that if this woman who was totally blind could believe this truth, then it must be so. I tucked away her nugget of wisdom for a time when I might need it. Yet hoping I wouldn't, for a very long time. Little did I know how valuable it would become.

Fast forward to the summer of 2013, with my recovery from tick diseases, and our concern for Anders. Through it all God was showing us that indeed our souls could be well in spite of difficult circumstances. Friends and family continued to be gracious and kind, reaching out with cards, putting us on their prayer lists, bringing our family meals and stopping by to cheer us up. One incredible gesture came from our wonderful friends the Stenbergs; a family who lived next door to us. We have a unique and special relationship with them and our children play with theirs just about every day. There are three well-worn paths between our homes, and our families share a meal together often. We joke that when our kids are old enough to date, they probably *won't* consider the Stenbergs because they're more like siblings to them. That's the kind of close relationship we have.

That summer, the Stenbergs asked us to join them for a family vacation on a houseboat fishing trip up in northern Minnesota. It was a chance of a lifetime for us. Fishing was an activity our whole family enjoyed doing together and the lake we were headed to was known as one of Minnesota's premier fishing spots; Rainy Lake. This gave us something to look forward to in the coming weeks. We could hardly wait! But in the meantime, we had a few more doctor appointments to get through.

It was advised by several other CF families that we should consider transferring our care to the University of Minnesota. Thanks to Melissa, we were connected with one of the best in the field, a specialist by the name of Dr. Warren Regelmann who was also the co-director of the Cystic Fibrosis Center at the U of M. Thankfully, we wouldn't need to wait long to see him. He was able to fit Anders into his schedule almost immediately. We made plans to bring the whole family along including Nathan's mom, and not because we were all so anxious to meet this new guy. Cystic Fibrosis is hereditary, and since we knew Anders had CF, it was possible that Carson and Ella could have it too. Although, it seemed highly unlikely, considering neither of them appeared symptomatic. There was also a chance that they could be a carrier of one of the mutations. Our children needed this for when they got married and decided to start a family in the future.

At that time, our son Carson was eleven and entering sixth grade and Ella, our daughter, was nine and going into fourth grade. We felt that Carson was old enough to know most of what Anders was potentially facing. We didn't share all of the details, but offered to answer any questions he might have. With Ella, we tried to be much more careful in sheltering her from the frightening truths of the disease. Although, it was not easy as she was our most inquisitive child, wanting to know details.

Soon we found ourselves in downtown Minneapolis at the University of Minnesota Children's Hospital. It was another long day of examinations, scans, x-rays, poking, and prodding; even more so than usual because it was a new hospital and of course they wanted to have their own samples and information.

Not once did I regret making the switch. From the moment we stepped inside I felt like we had entered a facility with innovative expertise and excellence. It was also a teaching hospital and I appreciated that. I could tell that Carson and Ella were nervous about having to give blood samples. However, knowing that their little brother did it all the time caused them to put on their best, brave faces.

Finally, it was time for our consultation with the respected Dr. Regelmann. Nathan's mom took Carson and Ella downstairs to a special commons area, while Nathan and I remained with Anders for some one-on-one time with the doctor. This man had been around a long time and was renowned for his knowledge and experience with CF. As he sat before us looking over Anders' records and results, I was sort of shocked to see him literally scratch his head and give a long, "Hmm…" He was quiet for about three or four minutes, although it felt like twenty, and I tried not to stir in my chair. The doctor was wise and I wanted to be still and let him analyze the data. At last, he began his consultation.

"Well, this is certainly an interesting case. I'm not sure if you realize it, but your son's mutations are quite rare. In fact, there is only one other reported case like his in the world. That means we really don't know much about it. I can't tell you how quickly his CF will progress because there is only one documented case to compare."

We were stunned, but we appreciated his honesty. This expert wasn't going to try and pretend he knew it all even with his years of practice and capability. My son's case was unique. In fact this was the reason Anders' newborn screening came back negative. His CF mutations were so rare, they went undetected.

The doctor continued, "At this point, I'm going to diagnose Anders with atypical Cystic Fibrosis. I see signs in his CT scan of acute sinusitis so I'll prescribe treatment for that. I'd like him to continue with all of his current medications and hold off on the airway clearance therapy for now. Let's have him re-evaluated for his progress with CF in a few months. When he comes back, we'll do another sweat test, pulmonary function test and discuss the results."

The doctor spent a significant amount of time answering our questions and helping us gain better understanding of this complicated disease. We learned we would need to make adjustments in our household including finding various hypoallergenic materials for Anders and become more conscious about preventing germs and infection. A dietician came in to speak with us about proper nutrition for CF patients. We would need to make some changes in Anders' diet by adding a higher content of fat, sodium and more calories. Various supplements and foods like sour cream, extra butter and salt, along with additional snacks throughout the day would help meet his need to gain weight. We laughed a bit at that, knowing Anders probably wouldn't mind this change one bit. Finally, we were assigned a social worker. She was a sweet young woman who offered us great materials regarding CF at school and home. One item was a beautiful hardcover children's story book about a little girl with CF titled, *Who I Am!* I flipped through it briefly and knew this would be a terrific resource to use with our kids.

As we stood and prepared to leave, we were reminded that the lab would call us in three weeks with results on Carson and Ella. I looked at my calendar and realized we'd be on our houseboat trip during that time. I circled the approximate dates in my calendar so I wouldn't forget, though I doubted that would happen. We gathered up our family and decided to treat everyone to pizza for supper. It had been a long day.

For the next couple of weeks, life returned to some normalcy and it was good. We needed ordinary days. Anders was experiencing a period of time without any sickness and my own health was at nearly 100%. We planned for our upcoming houseboat trip and looked forward to getting away from it all. I soon learned that getting away also meant no internet and spotty cellphone coverage, since the lake we were headed to bordered Canada and complete wilderness. *What?* I thought. My cellphone was like another part of my body and I wasn't sure how I could survive an entire week without it. I would just have to read books or something, I laughed.

Then it hit me. What about the lab findings? I was supposed to know something about Carson and Ella's test results that same week. I tried to tell myself it wouldn't be a big deal. So what if I had to wait a few extra days on the genetic testing results for Carson and Ella. We didn't really expect to hear disappointing news regarding them anyway. The testing was mostly for precautionary measure.

The trip was going to be especially exciting because we kept one important element from the kids. All they knew is that it was going to be a camping trip; the houseboat part was a complete surprise! It was hard to keep it a secret but totally worth the anticipation. The six hour drive to Rainy Lake was long to be sure. Traveling with seven children ranging in ages three to eleven had its unique challenges. But we had enough books, DVD players, iPads, and snacks to keep them entertained and from going stir crazy. Finally, the moment arrived as we pulled into the parking lot of Northernaire Houseboats. There sat our home for the next seven days, a beautiful forty-five foot, two-story houseboat complete with full kitchen, bathroom, living room, sleeping for twelve, and a waterslide!

Our home for the week was a two story houseboat complete with waterslide.

"Hey kids, you see that big giant boat with the blue waterslide out the back? Well, that's going to be our camper for the week!" You could probably hear the squeals and shouts of our ecstatic children from across the enormous lake. This was going to be a blast!

The houseboat vacation lived up to its expectation and we were having a wonderful time. Our two families spent glorious days fishing, swimming, and exploring the countless islands that Rainy Lake had to offer. It was good therapy to laugh and be with friends. I didn't even miss having Facebook, email, or texting and I truly did get lost in a good book. I had taken along an old copy of *The Hiding Place* by Corrie ten Boom. It had been years since I read it and I thought it might be good to reread Corrie's inspiring true story of faith and courage through the worst of adversities. I found myself glued to the pages and completely captivated by her testimony.

Corrie was a Dutch Christian who, along with her father and sister Betsie, helped many Jews escape the Nazi Holocaust during World War II. Corrie and her family were imprisoned for their actions and this story described the ordeal.

One of my favorite parts of the book takes place in the notorious Ravensbruk Concentration Camp. Corrie and Betsie were prisoners there and found themselves trying to fall asleep one night amidst reeking straw-bed platforms swarming with fleas. Betsie had an incredibly optimistic, glass-half-full attitude. She gently reminded Corrie of their morning Bible reading which was from I Thessalonians 5:18, *"Give thanks in all circumstances; for this is the will of God in Christ Jesus."* I could just imagine Corrie looking around at the dark foul-aired room declaring, "Betsie, there's no way even God can make me grateful for a flea!" But Corrie eventually relented and together the sisters prayed and gave thanks to God for the fact that they were together. They thanked God that they had miraculously been able to smuggle in a Bible. They even thanked God for the crowds of prisoners, because more people would be able to hear God's Word. Then, much to Corrie's chagrin, Betsie thanked God for the fleas.

It turned out Betsie was right. Those fleas were indeed a nuisance, but also a blessing; because they were what kept the guards from serious inspection of the prisoners, allowing the women to have Bible studies in the barracks with a great deal of freedom. They were never bothered or harassed by their supervisors, who detested the fleas. *God's Word says to give thanks in all things*, I thought. Another comforting nugget of truth to tuck away and add to my growing pile.

Day five of our houseboat trip started out like all the rest. Our alarm clock that week was the call of a loon and the sway of the boat in the water. A beautiful sunrise sparkled like diamonds on the lake and gave an outlook for yet another glorious day. Several kids woke up already in their swim suits, probably having never taken them off from the previous day, and the smell of brewing coffee and frying pancakes drifted from the kitchen.

Suddenly, a strange chirping sound, somewhat like crickets came from the back room. It took me a second to realize it wasn't actual crickets, but my cell phone ringtone. It was on and charging in the back room because I had been using it as a camera all week. How in the world was I getting a signal out here? Ella reached it first and yelled,

"Mom it's the hospital calling!" That jerked me to attention immediately and I grabbed it from her. Running to the top of the houseboat as fast as I could in hopes of the best possible reception I quickly swiped to answer, praying I wouldn't lose the call. Miraculously, I heard a voice quite clear.

"Hi, I'm from the University of Minnesota Genetic Counseling clinic. Is this Carson and Ella Waterworth's Mom?" I was out of breath from running up a flight of stairs. I told her yes and how surprised I was to receive her call.

"It's possible I could lose you, as we're on a houseboat near the Canadian border and my signal is really poor." I said, winded. She told me she'd get right to the point then. With an almost automated tone of voice I was told that my daughter Ella did not have any CF mutations. She wasn't even a carrier.

"Thank you Jesus!" I thought to myself with relief. But with barely a break in her speech, the geneticist went on to say that Carson's results came back with the same exact findings as his brother Anders. Meaning he also had Cystic Fibrosis. Her words were overwhelming and I wasn't sure if I heard her correctly.

"I'm sorry, what did you say?" I stammered.

"Your son Carson needs to be seen by one of our CF specialists as soon as possible for an evaluation." I didn't say anything for a while. I was in shock.

"Mrs. Waterworth? Are you still there? Can I transfer you to our scheduling department?"

"No!" I wanted to shout. I wasn't ready for this news. I didn't want to be transferred to scheduling. And then, something brought my attention to the lake and I looked up. There, out on the beautiful sparkling water was my son Carson. He was in his happiest place on earth; fishing in a kayak. He had no idea his world was about to be turned upside down. His only concern at that moment was trying to hook into a small mouth bass. Suddenly, the hymn, *"It is Well with my Soul"* popped into my mind and a calming presence and peace filled me. I took a deep breath.

This photo was taken just minutes after learning that Carson had CF.

"Yes, I'm still here. Go ahead and transfer me please. Thank you."

Just when I needed it, that first beautiful nugget of truth I had tucked away for just such a time as this came flooding back.

"Even if it is not well with our circumstances, it can still be well with our soul." I was on hold for only a few moments. Then, a kind man from the CF Care Center's scheduling department set me up with an appointment which would take place two days after we returned from our trip. Once the call was finished, I lingered on the top deck alone for a little while, just breathing in the summer air. The hymn, *It is Well with my Soul* was still going through my head.

When peace, like a river, attendeth my way,
When sorrows like sea billows roll;
Whatever my lot, Thou hast taught me to say,
It is well, it is well with my soul.

And then, I thought about Corrie and Betsie's willingness to thank God in all circumstances. Could I do that too? Bowing my head, I made the attempt.

"Thank you God for all three of my children. Thank you for miraculously allowing cellphone coverage so that I could receive this call." My last prayer was the hardest. It took me a moment to say it.

"And thank you that Anders is not alone in his CF journey."

Chapter 6

SUPERHEROES

T rials like the ones we were experiencing have the potential to put a lot of strain on a marriage and family. When worry or depression enters into a relationship, it can easily cause friction between a husband and wife and tear them apart. Miraculously, that didn't happen for Nathan and me. When I was down, God would give Nathan the strength to pull me up. And when Nathan was discouraged, I was able to muster the support he needed to put one foot in front of the other. We each had our different ways of coping. I would journal or go for long bike rides by myself. He would run on the treadmill early in the morning or read his Bible and pray. But we were there for each other like no one else could be because we fully understood what the other was going through. If anything, our difficulties brought us closer together than ever before. We clung to one another tightly.

When I told Nathan about Carson's unexpected results, we agreed that our son should know the truth right away. He was a sensitive boy and the more time he had to process this information before his impending doctor appointment, the better. Our houseboat trip would be coming to an end in just thirty-six hours. Then, two days later, we'd head to the CF clinic for Carson's first appointment with a specialist. Not a lot of time. So Nathan and I took Carson out fishing, just the three of us. It was then that we broke the news to him. Normally I am the one to communicate but I found myself too choked up to speak. So Nathan did the talking. I couldn't even look at my boy. I just stared out at the lake with tears running down my cheeks as Nathan told Carson the awful news. Our precious son took it so well. He was more worried about me than anything. He reached over and put his hand on my shoulder.

"Mom, are you going to be all right?" I grabbed his hand and nodded yes while stifling a sob. Being a parent was the hardest job on the planet. This was *not* one of those moments I imagined when Nathan and I decided to have a child!

Later, we took Ella out by herself in the same boat and told her of Carson's diagnosis. Her nurturing and maternal heart spoke volumes as she said to us through tears,

"I just want my brothers to be able to get married and have a family someday." Her words brought a fresh flood to my own eyes and we all cried together out on the lake.

It was a somber end to our houseboat vacation. And forty-eight hours later, our family was back at the University of Minnesota Children's Hospital meeting with the well-regarded Dr. Regelmann once again. It was an exhausting day as our oldest son underwent all of the same tests that Anders did, not long ago. But the news we were given that day left us feeling more devastated than ever before. There was no scratching of the head or uncertainty this time from the doctor. He seemed quite sure of what he had to tell us; and it left us stunned.

"Unlike Anders who I consider to be atypical, Carson has what I call full-blown Cystic Fibrosis. Carson's pulmonary function tests show some obstruction. That coupled with his chloride sweat test results indicate reason for him to begin airway clearance therapy immediately."

In layman's terms, this was not good news. It meant that Carson's CF was causing damage to his lungs and he needed to begin daily airway clearance therapy, known as "the Vest", as soon as possible. Everything was happening so fast! We were totally blown away. How could this be? Our son was seemingly healthy! And yet his CF was more progressed than Anders'? There must be some mistake. I found myself questioning everything we had been told, and then suddenly, I lost control of the situation and burst into tears. Normally, I don't cry in front of others but I couldn't help it. Carson just sat in his chair completely dumbstruck. Poor Nathan was in denial. Our room was soon flooded with additional medical staff. No time was wasted once it was determined what Carson's needs were. A respiratory therapist entered to orient us on the airway clearance system. But when she saw my tears she stopped in her tracks.

"Oh, I'm sorry, is this a bad time?" *Is there ever a good time for this?* I thought to myself. But I motioned for her to come in anyway, warning that we were in a state of shock and may have trouble comprehending her words and instructions. She was compassionate as she began her overview of the new pieces of medical equipment which would be entering our home in the next twenty-four hours. As she spoke, I glanced over at Carson. Awareness gradually washed over him. He literally began backing up in his chair, gripping the arm rests tightly while fighting tears.

"Wait, that thing is for me?" He said. "I have to wear *that*? What for? Mom, tell me what is going on?" He implored. His face was filled with absolute horror as he looked at me and then Nathan, pleading with his eyes for us to somehow rescue him from the entire situation. And more than anything I wanted to say,

"Honey, grab your things. We are leaving this hospital because this simply cannot be true. Let's go."

But I couldn't. Making my child remain seated in that chair felt like the most dreadful thing I could ever do to him. But I knew I had to. The respiratory therapist continued for another twenty minutes. I honestly don't remember much of what she told us. I do remember she was gentle and kind. She assured us that the thick folder of information she handed me would recap all of the instructions and an in-home therapist would be following up with us the next day to go over everything again.

There were many specialists that day. A dietician entered our room to discuss important nutrition facts for CF patients. After her speech, we were given another thick packet of information. Before fresh tears could begin, a lab technician entered to take another specimen from Carson. Then, a geneticist and her tag-along medical student came to ask us about being part of a case study and potential clinical trials. It literally felt like a three-ring circus in that hospital room.

Lastly, a social worker came to talk about support groups; school and CF care at home. She told us honestly,

"Nathan and Leanne, I'm not sure if you're aware but, it's recommended that people with CF should not be within six feet of other CF patients, in an effort to keep from cross infecting potentially harmful bacteria. Obviously with siblings this is impossible, but things like avoiding sharing a bedroom, bathroom, or dishes are some things to consider." She gave us more pamphlets and a three-ring binder. I had no idea. I began to think about how this might affect us. Anders had shared a room with Carson his entire life! Now what do we do? Finally, after a shattering and emotional experience we were free to leave, ending what felt like the worst day of my life. The looks on Nathan and Carson's faces told me it felt the same to them.

It was a quiet drive home. As I gazed out my window at the passing cars, whose occupants were completely oblivious to our pain, I felt shocked that the rest of the world could just go on as usual. I wished it would stop for at least a few minutes so we could catch our breath. People were commuting home from work, shopping, the DJs on the radio joked and ranted about things that had no importance whatsoever. I saw people outside, walking, eating, and enjoying the weather. Meanwhile, my life felt like it was spinning out of control.

I looked down at my phone to find several missed calls, voicemails, and text messages. Everyone wanted to know how the appointment went. At that moment I had no desire to talk to anyone at all, not even my parents. But I knew they deserved some kind of answer so I punched in a mass text to our closest family and friends simply saying,

"It was a long, difficult appointment. Carson has obstruction in lungs and begins Vest therapy immediately. More details later. Thank you for prayers."

I really struggled with having to send out that message because telling people validated the truth and made it seem real. Couldn't this still be just a terrible mistake? I mean, Anders was our sick one. His being diagnosed with CF was awful but at least it made sense. With him we had some kind of warning; some preparation. With Carson, we were completely blindsided. All this time, we had been telling him about Cystic Fibrosis because his little brother had it. We wanted him to know and understand. Now, the tables were turned and somehow he had it too? It felt so cruel! How does an eleven-year-old boy make sense of this? We were about to find out.

I'm not sure if anyone can say they look back on their time of adolescence or pre-teen years with fondness. It can be an awkward time in life when we're trying to fit into growing and changing bodies and figure out who we are, what we're good at and who will accept us. Add on top of that, a diagnosis of a life threatening illness. That's what Carson was dealing with just weeks before starting 6th grade. He was already anxious about entering middle school, and coupled with this news, he was absolutely certain his life was over; in more ways than one. Through gut wrenching sobs he told us,

"I just wish I had done something great with my life before all of this happened!" I prayed I could help him feel secure and believe he still had plenty of greatness to offer the world.

For a while, we had been praying about the possibility of sending Carson to a small private Christian School. With his personality, it seemed like a better fit for him than the public school our other children attended. When the diagnosis came, his desire to go there only increased. But tuition was high and we weren't sure how to make this happen financially. Of course, God did.

When I finally got around to listening to the voicemails on my phone from our long day at the hospital, one of them was from a dear friend. She wanted to discuss Carson's schooling of all things. It seemed strange and out of the blue and I was curious. She was the only person I called back that night. As it turned out, she and her husband had been prayerfully considering paying for Carson's tuition at school for the year! All this *before* they knew about what had taken place during the hospital that day. Amazing! Even in the midst of difficult circumstances, it was evident that God had His hand in the situation and was in totally control; even when I felt things were out of control. In astonishment and humility, we accepted our friend's generous offer and within a few days we found ourselves at Valley Christian School signing papers and registering Carson for class. Talk about a whirlwind of change for that sweet boy! But God was good, all the time. He was using His people to heroically encourage us.

Less than twenty-four hours after our appointment at the hospital, a FedEx truck came to our house with several large, heavy packages. Normally, it's exciting to have one of those big white trucks stop in front of your driveway. It can feel like Christmas, racing to open the long awaited shipment of online purchases. But this particular delivery left a sick feeling with us all. The boxes contained Carson's new airway clearance Vest, a compressor, tubing, a nebulizer machine, and all of the neb kits he would need to last him for the next six months. None of us hurried to open the boxes. In fact, we didn't even touch them. I just left them on the porch and tried not to look at them. Later that evening, an in-home respiratory therapist would come and show us how to set everything up. This machine, which cost more than my Volkswagen minivan, was soon going to take over my living room. I didn't mind if it stayed in its packaging a few more hours.

Even though none of us really wanted to, we knew we had to pay attention when we were given instructions on the Vest, the second time around. The therapist arrived right on schedule and Nathan and I welcomed her to our home. We chatted for a bit and then got down to business with the training session. My nursing skills as a mom kicked in and I took notes as she gave directions on programming the machine, troublingshooting and care. Carson was doing a pretty decent job of being civil during this time. You would have never guessed that he had a near temper tantrum right before the respiratory therapist arrived, which was very uncharacteristic for him. He was no angel-child, but I could probably count on one hand how many times he had ever put on a stomp-your-feet, scream and cry fit; even as a toddler. During supper that night, however, in a protest about not wanting to be present during the in-home Vest orientation, he slammed a milk glass down, spilling it everywhere while yelling defiantly,

"I am NOT DOING THIS. I hate CF!" Normally, this wouldn't fly in our household but considering the unique circumstances I calmly said,

"Sweetheart, why don't you go to your room and chill out for a while, okay? We'll talk about this later." He stomped off in defiance.

Remarkably, after a short time in his room, Carson pulled himself together. As he was fitted for the Vest, I could tell he felt awkward and insecure. As the therapist turned on the machine to its easiest setting, the Vest inflated and then his body began to slowly shake up and down. I placed my hand on his back so I could try to get a better understanding of what it felt like. It reminded me of a washing machine on the fastest spin cycle, even on this lowest setting. The sound of it resembled a helicopter nearby. When Carson spoke, his voice pulsated, like he was speaking into a fan, except with much more intensity. Carson blushed with embarrassment when he realized it. Nathan grinned and I could tell he was about to bust a gut but I shot him a look that said; "Don't you dare laugh". Surprisingly, Carson cracked a smile which eventually led to a quiet chuckle. This sounded funny because of the machine and that made us all start to giggle. Finally, we were all having a good laugh and it was a wonderful relief.

The therapist went on to show us some things about the

different settings while the machine continued to run. Carson would eventually need to work his way up to six higher levels over the course of thirty minutes. His therapy requirements were to do a half hour of vesting in the morning, and another half hour at night, along with his nebulizer. Finally, the therapist put the machine on pause giving Carson a break. Just a few minutes of him trying the Vest was exhausting and he said his stomach felt a little queasy. She suggested giving him some water to sip on. I decided to try the Vest on myself, so I could gain some perspective for what Carson would need to endure. It only took me thirty seconds and I wanted that thing off as feelings of claustrophobia and nausea arose. Even on the lowest setting, I felt it shake my entire core. It would certainly take some getting used to.

It was 9:30 PM by the time our in-home session was over and we were all outright exhausted. Once the kids were tucked into bed it was late. Nathan and I trudged up the stairs to our room and sat awake for a while with the lamp on, although we didn't really feel like talking much or watching anything on TV. We were basically just trying to digest everything that had taken place over the last few days, and process the realization that our lives would be forever changed. Suddenly, there was a soft knock on our bedroom door. We both looked at each other with a questioning gaze. It was Carson. He tentatively walked over to us and even though he was eleven, he appeared as a little boy. He asked if he could sit on our bed and talk to us. I turned down the covers and let him crawl in.

"Of course you can sweetheart. Ask us anything and we'll do our best to answer."

"Okay... Well, you know that vest thing?" He ventured. I raised my eyebrows with a curious look. How could we possibly forget?

Carson continued. "I was just wondering... Will I have to do that forever? Like, for the rest of my life?"

His words pierced my heart and I couldn't make eye contact with him anymore. I didn't know what to say. How in the world could I possibly tell him the truth? There was no cure for his disease.

It is progressive and he will always have to do his Vest therapy; every single day from now on, for the rest of his life. What an overwhelming thought. I couldn't tell him that! But thankfully, in that difficult moment God gave Nathan incredible wisdom. With gentle words, he came to my rescue, speaking tenderly to Carson.

"Honestly Bud, we really don't have the answer to that question. But doctors and scientists have come a long way with this disease. So who knows? Maybe someday all you'll need to do is take a pill and that will be it. But for now, your job is to stay healthy by doing Vest therapy every morning and every night and taking medicine that the doctors prescribe you. Can you do that? Until something changes?"

Carson gave a very heavy sigh that seemed to release the weight of the world on his shoulders. And then he said, "Okay, I'll do my best." I could only imagine how hard it was for him to muster those words. I was so proud of his strength. Together, the three of us hugged our son and stayed that way for a long while. I suddenly had a flashback to when he was very young and I used to rock him to sleep. He sure was growing up fast. And in that moment he became my hero.

A few weeks later I wrote this poem:

A Similar Road

It was the month of May, I remember the day,
When I saw you for the very first time.
Your eyes were blue, your fists were curled,
And your hair was soft and fine.
It felt so right, holding you tight,
I marveled at how perfect you seemed.
You made me a mom; you were my son.
I thanked God for all I had dreamed.
You quickly grew and time just flew!
We've been given so much to be proud of.
I get glimpses of manhood when I look at you,

As you show wisdom, patience and love.
God made you strong and it didn't take long
To learn the reason that you must be.
You were given an uphill battle to fight.
A diagnosis and new normalcy.
It seemed unfair when I'd see you there,
Taking on such a heavy load.
But I'm comforted to know that God's child too,
Walked down a similar road.
His only Son was the perfect One,
To take on the sins of the world.
He walked willingly to a cross on a hill,
God's plan for salvation unfurled.
Did God's heart break? Was it hard to take?
To see His child suffer and die.
Yes, He knows our pain and feels it the same.
He will never leave our side.
We all felt fear, but it soon became clear,
That God had His hand in it all.
He was present with us as we grieved and felt lost,
Promising to catch us when we fall.
I began to see His plan for me,
And how to make sense of the pain.
God can take even our darkest of days,
And use it for heaven's gain.
Someday there will be a new family,
Who will walk that similar road.
I want to be there to show them God's care,
Just as others have lightened our load.

All of us process and handle stress differently. I prefer to be active and not sit idle. I immediately began researching CF and what was being done to fight against it. Deep down I was hoping there was something I could do. I learned more about the disease, about the foundation, living with CF, and treatments. On the CF Foundation's website, I found a section that my hands-on, yes-girl type personality was drawn to. I clicked the "GET INVOLVED" link. In it I discovered the perfect outlet for me: *the Cycle for Life*.

In just two months, there was to be a twenty-five mile bike ride to raise awareness and funds for the Cystic Fibrosis Foundation. It was exactly what I needed. After all, I was already riding my bike regularly. Cycling was an activity I did to transfer my sadness and frustration into something physical instead of just letting it mull around in my mind. Now, riding my bike would actually serve more than just the purpose of relieving stress; I could literally be pedaling for a cure! I began to talk to friends and family about it and the idea spread like a wildfire. I realized that others had felt helpless while watching our family go through this process and when finally given an opportunity to do something tangible, they jumped at the chance. As I started brainstorming about a team name, a vision of Anders in his Superman costume, walking the hallways of Children's Hospital came to mind. The *CF Superheroes* was born. Soon, team members started signing up and donations poured in. I purchased blue CF awareness bracelets from the foundation for my family and cycling team members. The bracelets said "BREATHE" on them and we wore them with pride.

One day, I was contacted by a local, dear friend named Angie, who operates her own hand-made jewelry business called *Blossom Squared*. She approached me with the idea to create a beautiful square glass pendant necklace in blue or yellow, to coincide with the foundation's colors, displaying the word "breathe" on it. I loved the concept! Angie proceeded to make about one hundred jewelry pieces and gave them to me, at no charge, with the promise that I would sell them and donate all of the profits to our Cycle for Life fundraiser. I was blown away by her incredible generosity! This helped our efforts tremendously, and it also brought awareness to the cause. What a thoughtful friend she was. Angie was one of our heroes.

The cycle event, and everything that led up to it, was a wonderful way to bond our family, meet new people who were also dealing with CF, and share our faith in Christ. Because all of the time people kept asking us,

> "How do you manage to stay so strong in all of this?" Our answer was always the same. "Through it all God has been with us offering His peace, love, and hope. And we know that He can use even this for good."

Several newspapers, some local and a few from out of town, did write-ups about our family and the unique diagnoses and challenges we were facing. I was so grateful they always included the importance of our faith. One of my favorite quotes came from a full front page article in *The Inter-County Leader*, a local paper, published in September, 2013.

"If anything, CF makes my boys even more special. They have a soap box to stand on; something to advocate. I told Carson, "God must think we're really strong to be able to handle something like this. I can't wait to see how He's going to use you."

As the day of the bike event drew closer, I was asked by Chuck Richards from the foundation to give a pre-race speech. I didn't feel qualified to do so, being so new to the CF community. My boys had only been diagnosed just weeks ago. But I prayed, asking God to use me however He saw fit. I believe the Holy Spirit filled me with the right words to say and on the day of the event, I spoke with boldness. I wasn't afraid to share from my heart and from God's Word. Moments before the race, I saw tears from the audience as I told of the encouragement I felt from every dollar that had been raised. I also explained the hope and comfort we felt.

"I wouldn't ask to have a CF family, but I can honestly say that it has put us in a position where we see firsthand, how much people care, and how much God loves us. We are blessed." It was such an honor to be His vessel.

My Cycle for Life team, September 2013

In the end, it was an inspirational and rewarding day as the CF Superheroes rode bikes for Anders, Carson, and so many others fighting to live and breathe with Cystic Fibrosis. The cherry on top was that we became the highest fundraising team bringing in over $6,500! As the highest *individual* fundraiser, I was personally rewarded with a gorgeously restored, blue and yellow antique bicycle cruiser, complete with a charming brown basket in front. As I walked up to take a look at my prize, I was in awe. It was beautiful! But honestly, I didn't need another bike. And, not to be impolite, but this particular one wasn't exactly my style. I was more into speed than big wicker baskets. As I looked it over and later thought about it on the way home, I knew exactly what I wanted to do with it. ...

I couldn't wait! Before arriving home after our long day with the Cycle for Life, I told Nathan to pull into my jewelry-making friend Angie's driveway. There, we presented an amazing superhero with a token of our appreciation.

Chapter 7

MEDICINE IN MANY FORMS

The Cycle for Life was definitely an uplifting event for us. We needed it, because staying positive felt like a full time job. Yes, we had eternal perspective and knew where our hope came from. But often our hearts were heavy; wading through our new normal felt so daunting sometimes. Carson was discouraged as he faced the realization of a life-threatening disease, learned to operate his Vest, nebulizer, and remembered to take his new medications. I was sanitizing medical equipment daily, keeping our house hypoallergenic and germ free, adding calories and sodium to the boys' diet, getting the kids off to school, plus trying to work my part time job, keep up with my volunteer responsibilities and with the kids' sports activities. Personally, I could feel depression sink in as summer faded into fall, although, during the day and in front of the kids I felt stronger. I could manage putting one foot in front of the other. But when the sun went down and darkness fell, I felt swallowed by its presence. Was it really true? Were my boys slowly deteriorating right in front of my eyes? I clung to scripture verses such as,

Psalm 34:18, *"The Lord is near to the brokenhearted and saves those who are crushed in spirit."*

Those words gave me security that God saw my pain and would rescue me. But I still felt plagued by intense sorrow. The worry I felt for my sons' future was so heavy at times, I didn't think I could get out from under it. I was plagued by questions. *How exactly would their CF progress? And when? In their teens? Their twenties? Would they need a lung transplant someday?*

In an effort to find tangible comfort, I actually dug out my childhood blanket from storage and slept with it at night. I knew feeling sad was a normal part of the grieving process. It had nothing to do with an absence of faith. But when sadness turned to depression and made it difficult for me to get out of bed in the morning, causing me to lose weight and my hair to fall out in clumps, I knew it was time to seek help from my doctor. Melissa was wonderful. My rock. She prescribed me an antidepressant. Eventually, I began to function more like myself. I wish there wasn't such a stigma against antidepressants; especially in the Christian community. Depression is more than a feeling of sorrow, a sign of weakness, or lack of trust in God. It is a medical illness that is treatable. I am so thankful that I saw my doctor regarding this struggle. Addressing the depression made me a better mom, wife, and person.

I also learned the importance of not looking too far into the future, instead focusing on each day as it comes. If I started considering what was ahead for our boys, the crippling fear and worry crept in. I realized that it was wrong to do that because who knows what life could bring. In twenty years, a cure could be found and our lives might be completely changed. Who knows? Only God does.

Another kind of medicine was a trip to my favorite salon. Nathan treated me to a professional massage and new hair style. Unfortunately, my hair-loss necessitated I get some inches, as in eight of them, taken off and layers put in. When the stylist turned my chair around for the big reveal, I admit I wasn't quite ready for just how short she had to go. If there was one favorite feature I actually liked about myself, it would have to be my strawberry blonde hair. I'd never dyed it. Ever. To see it now, completely butchered, left me devastated. Tears sprang to my eyes but I told myself, "Hair grows back and hats are in style." When Nathan saw me for the first time he exclaimed, "Wow! I love it!" He may have been stretching the truth, but I took his compliment with a deep breath of acceptance. We both agreed that during this time especially, we needed to do whatever it took to build up morale within our family. It was important to remain upbeat for each other and our kids. Not that we should be faking a positive attitude. But because our family was going through so many changes and uncertainty, we wanted to offer our kids specifically as much stability and hope as possible.

In that search for hope, I researched an organization called Hopekids. We were referred to them by another CF family. Hopekids is a non-profit, organization that provides ongoing events and activities for families that have children with a life-threatening illness. Their website states simply, "Hope is a powerful medicine." So in the midst of cancer treatments and scares, a family can experience some positive anticipation as they look forward to attending a Twin's baseball game together. Also, mom and dad might have the rare opportunity for a date night at the Chanhassen Dinner Theater. All of the experiences are free thanks to in-kind donations with the hope that families will be blessed and look forward to their next Hopekids event. It didn't take long and our family was accepted into the program. Soon, I was looking through the Hopekids event calendar at all of the wonderful opportunities our family could take part in. There were tickets to an amusement park, private movie theater showings, bowling, football games and more. And it was all free. I thought about how hard it had been lately for Nathan. He was struggling too and I worried about him. Maybe what we all needed was a day out as a family. So I signed up the five of us for a pre-season University of Minnesota Gopher football game at the brand new TCF stadium. When I received confirmation that everything was in order I called Nathan to tell him.

"I have something important to say and I want you to hear me out. This coming Saturday I have arranged for our family to attend a Gopher football game. I know you probably aren't in the mood for this but I don't care. We are all going to wear matching maroon and gold sweatshirts. We are going to cheer, yell and teach our kids the fight song even if it's only a pre-season game. We are going to buy over-priced nachos for Carson, cotton-candy for Ella, and a foam finger for Anders and smile and have fun no matter what. You got it?" There was silence on the other end.

"Honey? Are you still there?" I asked a bit sheepishly. Silence. Did I overstep a bit? Did I push too hard? Finally Nathan spoke these familiar words,

"Ski-U-Mah!" This being the slogan used to cheer on the U of M's athletic teams; I relaxed knowing he was on board. A few days later, our family was decked out in the university's classic colors and on our way to the game.

We had an unforgettable time. Ella, a gymnast, loved watching the team cheerleaders flip and do stunts. Anders decided that he wanted to play football for the Gopher's someday. Carson's new favorite food was mini-donuts dipped in nacho cheese. Nathan enjoyed getting to experience the new stadium on a beautiful fall day. I loved being with my family and not thinking about doctor appointments and sterilizing nebulizer cups. Another wonderful facet about the day was getting to meet other Hopekids families who were also attending the game. My boys got to see kids who were, like them, dealing with life threatening medical conditions. For some, it was more obvious. The kids who had cancer were hairless. The little girl in the wheel chair had some sort of traumatic brain injury. Then, there was the boy with a colostomy bag. I later explained to the kids what that was for. It was really good for them all to realize they weren't the only ones who had unique and difficult circumstances to deal with. Life was filled with ups and downs and everyone has their issues in some form or another. Whether it's a need for braces, glasses, a hearing aid, or extra help in math; no one is perfect. I emphasized the fact with the kids that God doesn't make mistakes. He created each child with purpose and intent and He can use any one of them for His glory. I believed that. Nathan did too. The hard part would be for our children, especially Anders and Carson to believe it as well.

Sadly, our oldest was slipping into a depression. Unlike me, he didn't want to admit this. It seemed so wrong for a boy of his age to be going through depressive feelings. He was only eleven! He should have been thinking about hanging out with friends, having an airsoft war in the backyard or fishing. But instead he began to withdraw and become moody. Things set him off easily and he was agitated over the littlest annoyances. He also started voicing hopeless thoughts that frightened me. It was more than just feeling sorry for himself. He said things like,

"Why would God create me if I'm not even expected to live a full life?" Or, "What is the point of doing well in school if I'm not going to live long enough to have a career?" I knew where he was coming from but these questions were not accurate. Things could change. We didn't know what his future would hold. We tried desperately to tell Carson about new treatments on the horizon and stories of CF patients who were surpassing the odds all the time- but it didn't matter. We shared scripture with him, and posted a favorite one on a card near his bed.

> Jeremiah 29:11, *"For I know the plans I have for you,' declares the Lord, 'plans to prosper you and not to harm you, plans to give you hope and a future.'"*

However, these Bible verses about God's purpose and plan for him didn't penetrate his heart or change his emotions. Instead, he talked of wanting to end his life sooner than later. I can't even fully express how painful it was, as a mother, to hear my own child talk of wanting to die. To hear him say that his life didn't matter, it crushed me. Here was my son, the most beautiful, remarkable thing I'd ever done in my life, wanting death. He was such an incredible person. I could see it. Why couldn't he? I wanted to shake him and somehow make him understand that he needed to choose life, one breath at a time.

"Carson, don't you realize what an absolutely awesome kid you are? God has great things in mind for your future and I can't wait to watch you grow up and see you be used by Him!" But when mom's do that to their kids they get an eye-roll and a,

"Yeah, but you *have* to say that because you're my mom."

We made our social worker from the CF clinic aware of Carson's struggles and after some discussion it was decided to seek family counseling. Carson did not appreciate this idea one bit but we knew it was absolutely necessary. I tried to explain it to him,

"Sometimes it helps to try and talk to someone you don't know. You will be able to tell this person things without feeling judged and you can trust that it is completely safe. The hope is that they will provide you with some mental tools so that when you're really sad, and awful feelings or questions come up, you will know how to handle it better. It's important that your *entire* body is healthy- your lungs, your digestive system, and even your thoughts. Does that make sense?" With reluctance, Carson agreed.

We found a wonderful counselor who practiced locally in St. Croix Falls and together, Carson and I began seeing her regularly that fall. It was just one of the many forms of medicine that strengthened us on the road to good health while adjusting to a new normal and life with CF.

As fall progressed into winter, our learning curve was slowly increasing. Anders still had occasional illness and required a few visits with our primary physician along with antibiotics. Carson continued to struggle emotionally but he was open with us about his feelings, even though they were pretty much always negative.

God never stopped showing us constant love and faithfulness through his people as my husband's family put on a benefit for us in early November. We had incurred some costs with our modifications to life with CF and Nathan's dad's side of the family wanted to do something to help. So we made the seven hour drive north to the small town of New Folden, Minnesota, where Nathan's Aunt Teri cooked up a marvelous turkey dinner with all of the trimmings at the local community center. We were in awe as hundreds of folks in Nathan's dad's hometown came to show their support and generosity. Nathan and I personally didn't know many of these people, but they came in droves to show our family love. A local TV news crew, WDAZ channel 8 out of Grand Forks, North Dakota even surprised us by showing up to cover the story. After all, this was a big deal for a town with a population of just over 350.

It felt very humbling, and even a little awkward, to find ourselves the center of attention at an event such as this. We've attended benefits and fundraisers for *other* people, but obviously never as the recipients. However, folks wanted to help and I know it blessed them as it did us. I could see the pride in their eyes as they witnessed their community coming together to help a family in need. There were many tears, hugs, and promises of prayers from those who came. And through the event we were beginning to see glimpses of how God might be using our situation for his good as Nathan and I were able to share our faith and reliance upon God several times. The TV reporter came right out and asked us during a private on-camera interview what it was that gave us hope during these difficult diagnoses. We looked at each other with a smile and said without hesitation,

"Our faith and trust in God is what gives us hope. He helps us put one foot in front of the other. What we've learned through these diagnoses is just how precious life is and now, we cherish our family time even more." The story was aired later that night on the 5:00 PM, 6:00 PM and 10:00 PM news. God was definitely using this situation for His purposes.

Not long after that event, we found ourselves reporting back to the University of Minnesota Children's Hospital so Anders could be reevaluated. Every time one of these visits loomed, I found my stomach twisting up in knots. However, I was going to have to get used to this because from now on, our boys would require CF check-ups, every twelve weeks. During this particular appointment Nathan came along too. We were both on edge. Anders seemed totally clueless as he charmed us during yet another sweat chloride test. I decided to pull out my phone and take some video footage of him explaining the thirty-five minute process of sweat stimulation and collection, as best as a six-year-old can describe.

Even though our appointments were usually stressful and emotional, I wanted to use the opportunities to learn more about CF and help our kids, extended family, friends, and community understand it better too. If I could somehow capture our experiences and turn them into an educational opportunity I would. Sometimes I would take a picture or video of Anders or Carson undergoing a procedure or treatment and then share some background knowledge or medical explanation of it in a post on Facebook, Twitter, and Instagram or on my blog. Bringing awareness to this rare and complicated disease became very important to me.

"So Anders, when you have the sweat test done, do you need to use deodorant?" I teased him. He sat in a chair with little red and black apparatuses attached to his wrists. To me, they resembled a cheap children's watch with tiny tubes connected. He was putting on the charm in front of the camera as he raised one eyebrow at me, and made funny faces.

"No mom. It's taking my sweat out to see how salty it is. The sweat goes into this tube thingy here and if it's salty then the doctors can see if it has CF in it and I can get medicine and stuff and maybe a Vest." My kindergartener was learning things some people wouldn't hear unless they went to nursing school. I felt pride and sadness all at the same time.

It was about an hour later, sitting in a room with the CF specialist, that we learned Anders' sweat test numbers had gone up since our last time, meaning he was no longer atypical. Anders had progressed to full-blown CF, just like Carson, in a matter of a few months. He would need to start Vest therapy as soon as possible. The news didn't feel as shocking as with Carson and yet it was still painful to hear. It meant that Anders' disease was progressing. More medical equipment would be entering our home. Double the treatments, prescriptions, and hours of daily therapy. But this time, to soften the disappointment, we had a son who reacted on the opposite spectrum. Anders was completely elated!

"I get to have my very own Vest? Awesome! I'm gonna be just like Carson now!" Anders already knew what color he wanted for his Vest. "I want camouflage! Can I? Please?" Nathan and I looked at each other and considered the need to pull back on the reigns of his excitement. In our minds we seriously questioned, wondering if it was healthy for him to be so thrilled at this news. I felt conflicted seeing him happy with this huge adjustment to his life and my heart ached. I almost wanted to say to him, "Sweetie, don't you realize you're not supposed to be excited about this? You've just been told your disease is getting worse. Having to do Vest therapy isn't good news! This therapy is for the rest of your life!"

Of course, I didn't say any of that. Instead, I received his eagerness and enthusiasm as a gift from God and encouraged Anders however I could. My baby boy was so proud and courageous. Somehow, someway, I would muster that courage too. Although, convincing our oldest son would be another story.

When we arrived home the goal was to reach Carson before Anders did. I wanted to prepare him and make sure he didn't burst his little brother's oversized bubble. But unfortunately I was too late.

"Carson, guess what? I went to the CF doctor and I get my very own Vest just like you!" I stood behind Anders, secretly gesturing to Carson with my *meanest-mom ever* eyes that he'd better be nice.

Anders continued with pride, "My Vest is going to be camouflage. Isn't that so cool Carson?"

My oldest looked at me incredulously. He couldn't believe Anders was actually happy about this. I nodded my head that what he was saying was true and then with a raise of my eyebrows I tried to communicate that Carson should try to show some encouragement to his little brother. But Carson refused to acknowledge and act on my suggestion. Instead, he said with a huff and a smirk,

"Don't worry dude, it won't take long and you'll hate it as much as I do." Then he stormed down to his room and slammed the door. I sighed as my heart sank. Thankfully, this didn't seem to bother Anders too much that I could tell as he had already decided to start looking for his sister Ella to tell her the "*good*" news. Meanwhile, I prayed for endurance and wisdom.

The next day a large priority mail shipment from FedEx arrived with Anders' new medical equipment. My six-year-old boy stood on the front porch with typical anticipation as four large boxes were placed before him. Quite the opposite set of emotions from the last time a delivery like this came to our house. The driver said, "Wow! Is it your birthday or something Buddy?" I didn't know what to say in response and quite honestly I didn't feel like explaining. But Anders did.

"No, my birthday is February second. This is my Vest for CF so now I'll be just like Carson but mine will be camouflage."

"Oh, that's cool." The driver said a bit confused. I could tell he had no clue what Anders was talking about. I felt obligated to expand. I knew it was yet another opportunity God was giving me to bring awareness to CF and share my faith, so it was important to grab these moments. Sometimes though, I felt downcast and just didn't feel like talking about it. But as I spoke, the driver stopped, looked me in the eye, and really listened to my words; unusual for a typical, tightly wound FedEx delivery person who is always on a schedule. I prayed that he would not be left disheartened by the story of our diagnosis, but instead, encouraged by our faith in God's promises.

At the insistence of Anders, we brought the boxes into our house and opened them immediately. He couldn't wait to try on his new Vest. In reality, there was no need to be in a hurry to get all of his medical equipment out and I was certainly not in a rush to fill my living room with more or begin this new life routine. The in-home respiratory therapist wasn't coming for another two days. Frustration filled me at the thought of another medical professional needing to come again; it seemed pointless and a waste of time and money. Obviously we already knew how to operate the Vest. But it was proper protocol and included in the medical order to have someone conduct an orientation. So, forty-eight hours later we somewhat reluctantly welcomed another therapist into our home. Carson was very upset that we had to do this all over again. At supper that evening it was almost a repeat of his temper tantrum from last time. He told us emphatically that he did not want to be around when the therapist came.

"You cannot make me sit and watch Anders learn about this stupid Vest. I'm so sick of it!" He said with a challenging tone of voice. He was pushing the limits with his words and attitude. Nathan parented.

"Carson, first of all, it is not okay to talk like that to your family. We understand that this is painful and it's alright to feel upset. But it is not okay to take it out on us. Secondly, Anders is really hoping you'll be there to support him. But if it's going to be too hard for you, we understand and you can find something else to do instead."

As soon as we were finished eating and the dishes were cleared he went into his room and slammed the door. Ella remained and showed genuine anticipation for Anders.

"Do you think I could try your Vest on tonight when the therapist comes?" She asked him tentatively. She wanted to learn it all.

"Sure Ella!" He said proudly. It was refreshing to have Anders be open and willing to share this experience with us. Carson had been so self-conscious, he didn't want anyone to even ask questions about it, let alone be around when he was doing his therapy.

When the therapist finally arrived, we began with introductions as she was different than the first one who came when Carson was being orientated. Nathan, Anders, Ella and I all gathered with her on the living room floor with the Vest equipment spread out.

Anders wasted no time in immediately fitting himself with the Vest and plugging in the tubes to the compressor. The therapist quickly caught on that we were already familiar with the machine. I explained that we also had an older son with CF who was in his room reading. Realization came over her.

"Oh wow… You have two children with Cystic Fibrosis? I had no idea. Having one child with CF is hard enough, but two? I can't imagine how difficult that must be keeping up with all of the therapy, medications and doctor appointments. That's going to be like a full-time job for you." And then she got quiet and even choked-up. Looking at me and then Nathan, she asked, "How are you getting through all of this?"

I comforted her by sharing our belief that God was in control, even when things were tough.

"It has certainly been a difficult adjustment for our family. We've done a lot of praying in the last few months, but we have a strong faith in God and believe there is a plan in all of this." She pondered my words and I knew that once again this was an opportunity to share about our complete reliance on The Lord. However, Anders wasn't interested in letting us get too far off track. He was extremely anxious to get started with his very first therapy session.

"Can we push start now, *please*?" He had his Vest on and was ready to go.

"Okay Bubba." I smiled at my boy. Bubba was a term of endearment we had for him ever since he was a baby. "We can push start now."

Ella scooted over so that she was right by him with her hand on his back. She wanted to feel it inflate. The therapist smiled at Anders' and Ella's enthusiasm. I'm pretty sure she had never seen two kids so excited about the Vest before. And then out of the corner of my eye I noticed Carson standing in the hallway watching us. I nudged Nathan and then subtly nodded in the direction of our oldest son. I'm not sure how long he had been there, but we didn't say anything;

allowing Carson to decide when he was comfortable enough to come and join us.

The therapist programmed the machine and soon the Vest inflated with air. A few seconds later, the machine began to compress Anders lungs, faster and faster, causing his body to shake. I saw his face go from excited to suddenly apprehensive. Carson had been watching Anders the entire time. When he saw his little brother begin to appear anxious, that's when he made his move and came to the rescue. Carson immediately sat next to him, bringing along his most prized possession, his iPod. Big brother snuggled in next to little brother while tenderly putting an arm around him and said,

**As Anders tried out his new Vest, Carson
comforted him in a way none of us could.**

"Here Anders, this is what I like to do when I'm doing my treatment." And he let him play a game of Minecraft. It might sound silly, but to me, it was the most selfless gesture I'd ever seen Carson do. I was proud as I watched a miracle occur in my oldest son's heart that night. The sorrow for himself was beautifully replaced with empathy for his little brother. Carson knew exactly how hard this new life-change would be for Anders. Nathan and I watched him grow up right before our eyes as he took his role of big brother very seriously and did exactly what was necessary. Carson gave Anders something that none of us could offer: understanding, approval, comfort, and kinship. In a subtle way, Anders provided Carson with those things as well. They both had someone who could truly understand what the other was going through. I recalled my reluctant prayer of thanksgiving on top of the houseboat last summer.

"Thank you God that Anders is not alone in his CF journey."

Little did I realize that Carson would need his younger brother just as much as Anders needed him. My boys needed each other and God knew that. Having the two of them diagnosed was truly a blessing in disguise. I saw that now.

> Ecclesiastes 4:9-10, *"Two are better than one because they have a better return for their work. If one falls down, his friend can help him up..."*

Chapter 8

HIGHS AND LOWS

inter was back in full force and I wasn't happy about it. Anders was struggling off and on with sickness. Even with the Vest therapy and CF medications, it was still an uphill battle. At Christmas time, we had to rush him to the ER directly from a family gathering because we couldn't get him to stop coughing for thirty minutes straight. When the vomiting started, I worried he wouldn't be able to catch a breath. At the hospital they finally got him calmed down and his oxygen levels back to normal. During his next appointment at the University of Minnesota, they changed some of his prescriptions and I found myself being taught to use a syringe in order to administer his new medications. I was kind of proud being able to add that to my skillset as a mom. *I totally could have been a nurse!* I thought.

We were adjusting to yet another new normal as the amount of nebulizer cups and medications doubled. I remembered back to the days when simply getting my kids to take a bath and brush their teeth before bed felt like such a difficult chore. Now, those days seemed like a breeze. The long list of therapies and medications a person with CF does, in order to live to age forty, goes way beyond dental care. I wished our family could relive those easy mornings and nights; before CF was diagnosed. To simply let them sleep in again. Or allow them to stay out and play a little longer in the evenings with their friends. They missed that and I did too. But instead we woke them two hours before school started. It's still dark out at that time and Anders isn't a morning person. I pried him out from under his warm covers. He still had bedhead and I usually helped him get his Vest on. He wanted to snuggle with his stuffed animals as I handed him his first nebulizer. He would still be half asleep as his airway clearance Vest shook his entire body, moved the mucus out of his lungs, and forced him to cough; helping him to live longer. People didn't see it. Our boys might have appeared healthy on the outside. And that's a good thing. However, the stack of nebulizer cups that I forever washed and sterilized on a daily basis, the bottles of pills on our counter, the medicine in our fridge, and the machines in their room were hard to hide.

I was making multiple trips to our local drug store every week. Our boys were going through approximately $7,000 worth of medications on a monthly basis. Although, stopping in to our small town pharmacy, Tangen Drug wasn't so bad. The staff was kind and supportive and soon we got to know each other on a first name basis. I loved our little community! Most important, the treatments were making a difference in the boys' health. Carson's pulmonary lung function had improved by 10% since he started vesting. And medications like Pulmozyme and Mucomyst were life altering for Anders. The hard work was paying off.

With the recommendations from our CF Care Team, it was Nathan's goal to build Carson his own bedroom. Obviously it was impossible to keep our boys completely separated from one another, but there were some measures we could take in order to help prevent cross contamination of possible bacteria. Splitting up the boys into their own rooms was a start. Anders was having a hard time with this because his entire life he had shared a room with his big brother. He looked up to Carson so much and practically begged us not to let him move out. This tugged at my heart but ultimately I knew it was best for both boys. Carson was growing up, and having his own space would be good for him. He said he didn't really care, but my hope was that this would help lift his spirits and eventually he would get involved in the planning of his new bedroom.

Nathan, being a carpenter, had some great ideas to customize and design a unique area which reflected Carson's passion for fishing and hunting. And when it was all done, his bedroom looked like a gorgeous, Northwood's rustic cabin complete with rough sawn knotty pine paneling on the walls, a sliding barn style door for his closet, and against the opposite wall, a rod holder for his fishing poles. He had a log bed, a deer antler lamp, and an oversized chair with outdoorsy fabric; all furniture I proudly scooped up at garage sales. Just before the big reveal, I had filled rustic frames with photographs of Carson's favorite angling memories and placed them along the walls. His room was a fisherman's dream come true; a real man cave. When he was finally able to move in, I saw a dimple appear in his cheek, the one that only comes out when a real, genuine smile occurs. It was so good to see. He hugged his dad tight and then we gave him a chance to settle in. Ella and Anders also received a slight bedroom makeover so they were not excluded from the fun. Rearranging furniture and adding touches with wall decals and lamp shades can make a big difference. However, Anders needed a bit more convincing about the joys of having his own room. He also received a new stuffed animal and one more night light. He was going to miss having a roommate.

Having a little brother like Anders, who could understand the burden of treatments and medications, made a huge difference in Carson. But it definitely wasn't the cure-all for his depression. One area where I could see major differences in the way the two boys handled their CF was that Anders was so completely open about his Vest therapy whereas Carson was very private. It almost angered Carson that Anders would let anyone sit and watch while he vested. Anders acted as if it was the most natural thing in the world to sit and play LEGOs while doing his treatment; his friends or family staying to observe out of curiosity. But after a few minutes his buddies got over the strangeness of the machine and started building LEGOs too.

Carson was incredulous at the thought. One time, when Carson was doing Vest treatment in his room, Ella's friend came over and accidentally walked in on him. He was absolutely mortified. I honestly don't even think she saw anything nor would she have really cared but it caused Carson such agony, he immediately shut off his machine, ripped off his Vest, and yelled for me to come down to his room. As I quickly ran down the stairs, Ella's friend fearfully ran past me and I guessed at what had taken place. As I reached his bedroom I got there just in time to witness him kick his $12,000 airway compressor in a fit of anger. Obviously, this was totally unacceptable behavior but I saw so much pain and anguish in his face; it was hard to scold him. In fact, there were times when I felt like giving that machine a good swift kick myself! I'll never forget his mournful cries as he wept bitterly that day. He hated his life and how different he felt from his peers. Just the sound of that machine put a lump in *my* throat every single day. I couldn't imagine how he felt having to use it. I wrapped my arms around him, rocking him as I prayed aloud, "God, please reveal your plan to my son. He needs to see some good in all of this. Please." It was at this lowest point that I finally made the decision to contact the Make-A-Wish Foundation. I was told by our physician and several other CF families that we would qualify. But I didn't think we should pursue it. However, I soon realized that my son desperately needed something tangible to hope for; a positive distraction from the difficulties of treatments. He needed to dream and imagine a positive future. Maybe this was the answer? After a long heart-to-heart talk with Carson and a check on Ella's friend, I went to my computer and researched the application process for Make-A-Wish.

Nathan was struggling with how to help his boys too. As a carpenter and the main provider in our family, he just wanted to fix things and in this situation he couldn't. No amount of money, words, or hours on the job seemed to make a difference. We prayed and cried together often. One day a childhood friend of his named Kenton Rowe called somewhat out of the blue to catch up. They hadn't spoken in years. Nathan had grown up with this friend in Nebraska from about the age of four until twelve. And then, Kenton's family moved away to Ecuador to become fulltime missionaries. This was really difficult for Nathan and he recalls saying to his mom, "I don't know how I'm going to make it without Kenton. He's my strongest friend." Somehow, over the years the two boys remained friends and now, in their late thirties they reminisced about old times. Kenton was married and living with his wife and kids in Helena, Montana as a successful international wildlife photographer, shooting for *National Geographic* and *Nature Conservancy*. As they caught up on each other's lives, the conversation turned and Nathan found himself breaking down emotionally with Kenton as he shared about Carson and Anders and the difficult diagnoses. Kenton was a compassionate listener as Nathan talked for a while longer. It ended up being a good way for Nathan to release some of his frustration and heartache. The only person he had ever shared those deep things with was me. I was thankful for Kenton's willingness to listen and be a friend to my husband after all those years. But what blew us away even more was Kenton's phone call one week later. ...

Nathan called me from work one day saying, "Do me a favor. Go on your computer and look up *Pine Butte Guest Ranch* in Choteau, Montana." I thought it was a strange and random request, especially for the middle of the day but I followed his directions. When I typed in the name, a website popped up for a dude ranch owned by the Nature Conservancy. Stunning photographs displayed an absolutely picturesque setting of log cabins with a backdrop of the Montana Rocky Mountain front. There were horses galore, endless postcard scenes with glacier lakes, crystal streams, and abundant wild flowers. My jaw dropped and I asked,

"Nathan, what is this place? It's amazing! But why am I looking at this website?"

"Well, Kenton just called me and he wants to send our family to this ranch for a week-long vacation." There was silence for a few seconds as I let that sink in. But it still wasn't making any sense to me.

"Wait, what? Why? How? Nathan, I don't understand. Can you please tell me what's going on?" I could tell Nathan was giddy with excitement as he eventually went into a more detailed explanation.

"Kenton puts on photography workshops for the Pine Butte Guest Ranch and part of his compensation is vacation time spent there. He wants to give us one of his weeks of vacation. It's all inclusive and we just need to call and pick the dates!" Realization began to creep in as I scrolled through more photos of this incredible dude ranch. It was an absolute dream come true; a fantasy land for horse-lovers like Ella and me. And it would offer plenty of enjoyment for Nathan and the boys who would be free to hike and explore trout fishing in glacier lakes and mountain streams. Never in my wildest dreams had I ever imagined being able to take such a trip. And it was all because of the thoughtfulness and generosity of Kenton and his family.

"Are you kidding me? I can't believe it! This is amazing!" I said incredulously.

Nathan continued. "Kenton told me, he actually felt led by God to do this for us. He wants us to have some quality time as a family." I was stunned. We both were, really. The thought of a gift like that was hard to wrap our minds around. But it sure was fun to try! Eventually, I called the ranch and booked our family for the last week in July 2014. This gave us several months of anticipation and time to find our inner cowboy. Yee haw!

In the midst of everything happening with the boys, it was evident that our daughter Ella struggled somewhat to find her fit. She was a passionate young girl who was full of life and cared deeply about her family. She wanted to help, attend doctor appointments, always be in the know of what was going on, and to be noticed. When we did our Cycle for Life event she asked if she could participate. Ella was an exceptional athlete and I had no doubt that she could complete twenty-five miles of biking. Being a competitive gymnast, she trained eight to ten hours a week and was in better shape than I was. But the foundation had restriction limiting those under the age of eighteen to participate. Thus Ella wasn't allowed to join my team. However, she *was* invited to set up camp at one of the many rest stops along the route and be a cheerleader. On the day of the bike ride, she dressed up in a superhero costume and did back handsprings and cartwheels while cyclists went by. She was an absolute hit! That was our Ella, encouraging people wherever she went.

But she wanted to do more. When she heard me talking about another possible fundraising event scheduled later that winter called the CF Stair Climb, she asked if she could do it too. It was a unique, grueling experience where participants climbed fifty stories of the IDS tower in downtown Minneapolis to raise awareness and funds toward a cure for Cystic Fibrosis. Some extreme climbers even did it with firefighter gear on. I was still in the "maybe" stage when I called the CF Foundation to inquire about children participating in the climb. When I learned that there was no age restriction for this event, Ella was ecstatic! I was still hesitant.

"Honey, are you sure this is something you want to do? Fifty stories is *a lot* of stairs Ella." I knew when the words came out of my mouth it was a waste of breath.

"It's 1,250 stairs to be exact Mom. I already read about it in on their website. And yes I'm positive. It sounds like so much fun! Please Mom *please* can I climb too?" There seemed to be no deterring her. She was a very strong minded nine-year-old and this *was* a good cause so I relented. Before long, she was working on her personal online fundraising page, complete with pictures and a persuasive pitch.

Coincidentally, the CF Stair Climb was perfectly timed with a research project that Ella was expected to write with a partner in her fourth-grade class. Ella had a while to contemplate her chosen topic and who she wanted to work with. But apparently she was struggling with this and didn't tell me. Instead, she went to her teacher and said,

"Mrs. Fox, I know what I'd like to research, but I'm pretty sure no one in my class will want to be my partner."

The other kids in Ella's class were choosing subject matter like red-eyed tree frogs, Laura Ingalls Wilder, and volcanos. Ella had it on her heart to research the topic of Cystic Fibrosis. Most of her classmates would have a hard time pronouncing these complicated words let alone take an interest in learning more about it. But Ella did for obvious reasons. Thankfully, her teacher was gracious and compassionate, understanding why this was important. She allowed Ella to tackle the challenging subject matter without a partner. Ella got to work immediately and the elementary school librarian, Mrs. Platt, who knew this wouldn't be easy for a nine-year-old, offered some guidance and resources. When I found out that Ella had chosen CF for her paper I was really impressed. But there was also concern about certain information she would be learning. We had protected her from some of the difficult facts about CF, and I imagined that in her research, she would learn hard truths. The school librarian recognized this too and together, we decided to preview any materials or websites she used. But at the same time, allow Ella some room to learn and accept what is reality, even if it was difficult. I was so grateful for the support of our schools.

Over the next few weeks, as her paper and PowerPoint presentation came together, she also weaved in a plug for her CF Stair Climb fundraising campaign which, by the way, was doing incredible. Who wouldn't want to support and donate to an adorable little girl, raising money for charity? As the event drew closer, she raised almost $1,000 in pledges and recruited friends, teachers, and family members to join our CF Superheroes team. At home, she practiced giving oral recitations of her research project in front our family. The plan was for Ella to also incorporate a Vest demonstration in her speech. She blew me away with her confidence and ability.

On the day of her class presentation, with parents and grandparents filling the classroom, Nathan and I sat with tears threatening to fall. Emotions were mixed. One moment I was filled with pride as Ella stood at the podium, reading her report, which educated and raised awareness about a rare and complex illness. Then I felt sadness because this disease was about my boys. But things had changed a lot in the world of CF over the last fifty years and people needed to know. My little girl was making a difference.

~

In February of 2014, it was that time of year in our neck of the woods when the temperatures plunged way below zero and I repeatedly asked myself, "Why do I live in a place where the air hurts my face?" The polar vortex hit our small town of western Wisconsin with invincible force, making a simple trip through the grocery store parking lot feel like a difficult journey across the frozen tundra. Those that know me recognize that winter is my least favorite season. Every year at this time, I seriously considered moving our family to Florida. I did not appreciate the need for snow pants, insulated boots, earmuffs, hand warmers, waterproof fleece-lined gloves, mukluks, neck warmers, or long underwear. Every mom recognizes the challenges of putting a toddler into all of those necessary outdoor winter clothing items during the torturous season of potty training. I think my ancestors must have settled here in the month of June. But in a rather mortifying way, God taught me that my attitude is a decision, and I needed to consider being thankful in all things- even winter.

It was a frigid Saturday morning, and I was about to do Ella's hair, in preparation for one of her highly anticipated gymnastics meets, later that afternoon. She practiced long hours at Flex Gymnastics every week, all year round, and it came down to a few meets in the winter. This was what she trained for. Of course, the competition hair was pretty important too and I did a rather awe-inspiring French braided crown. We had already spent time scouring the internet for a unique and intricate idea for that day's meet. Armed with a water bottle, bobby-pins, hair spray and glitter, we were ready. Together,

Ella and I sat down on the floor of her bedroom and I got to work parting sections of her hair. It didn't take long however and I began to notice something peculiar; movement at the base of her scalp. I won't go into great detail because if I did, you'd probably start to itch and get that creepy crawly sensation while reading this chapter. I apologize to those readers who may experience any PTSD type symptoms. In fact, as I type, I'm fighting the urge to scratch my own scalp. That's what happens when people even mention the "L" word. Even though I'd never actually seen it firsthand before, I knew what it was the second I saw it. Lice! This being our first experience with the little buggers, I didn't know where to begin. So I did the logical thing. I called a fellow mom. Actually, it was my gracious mother-in-law, Marie, who received the panicky phone call. She lived just across the cul-de-sac from us. I knew she would be able to confirm it for me, being she was an experienced mom of four children. She came right over with a trusty magnifying glass, and sure enough, it was a positive diagnosis. My daughter had lice! Poor Ella immediately broke down in tears and I felt like joining her. But my practical side kicked in and I got right to work because all I could think about was that my home was being invaded by these nasty little creatures and I wanted them exterminated! Marie drove to Wal-Mart to get an anti-louse kit. I told her to buy several, just in case. Meanwhile, I went online to see about the best procedures for my household. Marie was already sharing remedies that included putting mayonnaise in our hair and placing bedding in plastic airtight trash bags for two weeks. I wanted to get my facts straight and potentially save myself some misery, but most importantly, make sure I killed those suckers! And then, while scanning different websites I came across this precious piece of information:

> *"To prevent the spread of lice, you may freeze items in temperatures of -5°F (-15°C) for 10 hours to kill lice and nits."*

Ah ha! I knew for a fact it was going to be even colder that very night! Suddenly, I found myself doing something I thought I'd never do, earnestly thanking The Lord for the subzero temperatures outside. I began grabbing bedding and pillows from everyone's room throughout the entire house and throwing it out on our front porch. I had no idea if anyone else was infected but I wasn't taking any chances. I was praising God for the season I usually loathed, while huffing and puffing from our upstairs bedrooms, to Carson's downstairs bedroom, lugging comforters, pillows, and sheets.

"I'm sorry Jesus that I always complain about winter and the freezing weather. Thank you, thank you, *thank* you for the cold outside! Please make all of the lice and nits freeze to death as soon as possible."

I'm not sure if that was a very holy prayer, but I can assure you it was a completely honest one from my heart.

Our other neighbors were probably wondering what in the world was going on at our house. Although, it may have appeared fun and festive, with all of the colorful household bedding and towels hanging across the railings, the porch swing, and several outdoor rocking chairs. I brought out every single pillow we owned along with all of the kids' stuffed animals; fifty-eight to be exact. My porch looked like the marriage of a garage sale and a quilt show. Marie arrived with the anti-louse kits and the shampooing, combing, and endless nit-picking process began.

After all was taken care of, the family joke was, "Mom can't hate winter anymore." I laughed along and agreed that it was true, realizing the situation would have been painstakingly longer had it occurred during a warmer season, other than the deep freeze. But I was also convicted by their comments. Here I was, trying to remain hopeful and be a positive example in the midst of CF, and yet at the same time, I had continued to hold a grudge against winter.

I realized that I had chosen a bad attitude in regard to our unavoidable weather. My kids were observing this behavior, and possibly even mirroring it. The Bible says,

I Thessalonians 5:18, *"Rejoice always, pray continually, give thanks in all circumstances, for this is God's will for you in Christ Jesus."*

That included the awful horrible diagnoses, the inconvenient weather patterns of February, and even a creepy crawly little bug invasion.

I needed to choose thankfulness, and not necessarily *for* all things but *in* all things. When I did this, the joy would follow. It's not the joy that makes us grateful. It is gratitude that makes us joyful. My hope and prayer was that if I lived this way, my kids would reflect it. I've since asked God to change my heart about the season of winter. I still don't like being cold. But now, I have a new appreciation for the diamond-like sparkles of snow in the trees, when the sun hits it just right. I enjoy the happiness on my kids' faces when a snow day is announced. And when the weather turns bitterly cold, I treat myself to a favorite hot beverage. No, you won't find me out snowshoeing or ice fishing with my husband and sons, but you will see me being more content during the winter months. I know that God has planted us here in St. Croix Falls for a reason, winter is *not* the end of the world, and He promises the mercy of spring.

～

The application process for Make-A-Wish went surprisingly fast and before long, both Carson and Anders were accepted into the program. The boys were soon matched with volunteers from the foundation called Wish Granters. Their names were Mike and Holly Jones and their responsibility was to get to know Carson and Anders and understand what their wish-come-true might be. They would convey this information to the Make-A-Wish board of directors who would make the ultimate decision. This was all done through application, interview, and spending personal time with our family. The boys were each mailed a thorough packet of information to fill out about by themselves. It asked them all kinds of questions ranging from their interests, favorite foods, and hobbies, to sports, animals, music and more. The packet also encouraged the boys to begin dreaming about their wish by offering different brainstorming activities. There was also a letter for parents that advised we shouldn't hold our children back, but instead, "allow them to think big and to dream." It was such a unique opportunity and a place we never expected to be. Our boys could basically ask for whatever they wanted; and it could quite possibly be given. It was mind-boggling!

On a side note, we'd been told many times throughout the Make-A-Wish process that "the boys deserved this." We'd heard this from friends, family, the Make-A-Wish staff, our doctors and the CF care team. But Nathan and I in *no way* wanted our kids to believe this was true. We quickly corrected anyone who said this; even if it was meant to be an encouragement.

"Actually, we don't feel this is in any way *deserved*. True, our family has been through extremely difficult circumstances. But all of us deal with trials in life. Unfortunately, there isn't a Make-A-Wish for job-loss, infertility, financial difficulties, or divorce. No, there is nothing we have done to deserve these wishes. It is all a tremendous *gift* that generous and thoughtful people have donated, to help brighten other people's lives and we will be forever grateful."

As Carson was going through his packet, I studied his reaction especially, because he was the initial reason why we had pursued this. When he reached the section where he could start writing thoughts and suggestions for a wish, he had only one thing in mind. He wanted a fishing boat. There wasn't anything else to consider. A trip to Disney World, meeting basketball legend LeBron James, or even receiving his own swimming pool could not compare. The only thing he ever wanted in the whole wide world was a boat. He looked at me with concern, wondering if that was too much to ask. I said with a smile, "You'd better write that one at the top, Bud!" However, in the back of my mind I felt slight concern. I recalled reading somewhere in the Make-A-Wish Wisconsin handbook that there were possible restrictions against motorized vehicles being granted; but the letter to parents specifically said, "Let your child think big." So for now, I decided to do just that.

With Anders, his ideas were a little more scattered. He was younger, having just turned seven, and this probably made a difference. He had many interests such as sports, animals, superheroes, and all things tropical, so it was a little harder to nail down a dream come true for him. The workbook packet seemed to be more useful for a kid like Anders. In one of his brainstorming activities he mentioned wanting to spend the day with the Minnesota Vikings running back, Adrian Peterson. On another page, he drew a picture of a dolphin swimming in the ocean and at the top of the page he wrote in crayon,

"I wish to have a dolphin for a pet." I wondered what Make-A-Wish could do with this kind of request? We would soon find out when Mike and Holly came to our house for first-time introductions. It was so exciting and felt like Christmas. Especially, when they came to our door carrying brightly wrapped gifts for all three of our children! This was something that really impressed me about Make-A-Wish. They made sure the entire family felt special and part of the experience. Ella had several packages with her name on them and she was thrilled. I was touched that she was also included in the interview process. We spent several hours together with Mike and Holly and by the end of the night both boys had their first, second, and third choices narrowed down, ready to submit to the foundation. It was recommended to have alternatives if for some reason their top choice didn't work out. Holly and Mike made sure that Carson especially understood this.

Anders	Carson
1st wish: Go to Hawaii and swim with dolphins	1st wish: To have a fishing boat
2nd wish: Play football with Adrian Peterson	2nd wish: Fish with a pro-fisherman
3rd wish: Be a superhero for a day	3rd wish: Go on a tropical cruise

Mike and Holly would present these, along with their personal recommendations, to the Make-A-Wish Board of trustees while we waited patiently. Meanwhile, the boys were each given a special wish token to keep, and whenever treatments or doctor appointments made life difficult for them, they could pull out that silver coin and remember a wish was coming soon. Both boys' faces lit up with expectation as they took the small shaped coin and turned it over in their hand. They each held it as if priceless. And to us all, it was.

Spring arrived, and normally, I would be feeling relief with a break in the weather. But that year we received tremendous amounts of rain. At first, it was nice because it cleared away the snow pretty quickly. However, we noticed that this was not good news for our basement. One afternoon, Carson and his buddy Calan were downstairs having a Nerf war when suddenly; they raced up to the kitchen wearing nervous looks on their faces.

"Dad, there's water downstairs! Some of our Nerf darts are floating in it!" Thankfully our basement was unfinished, but we had made it a usable space for the kids to play in. It was insulated and we had begun to install sheetrock on the walls. There were large carpet remnants and rugs, some gymnastics mats, and even a balance beam on the floor for Ella. Upstairs I tried to keep a clean, organized house but the basement was the one area where I could just shut the door and not worry about anyone seeing the disaster my kids and their friends had made with all of their toys. They had dress-up clothes, Barbies, baby dolls, a kitchen set, race tracks, match-box cars, Playmobile, Geotrax trains, and enough Nerf guns to supply an entire sixth grade class. Basically, it looked like Toys-R-Us had vomited down there! Now we were being told it was full of water?

Nathan and I charged down the stairs, and sure enough, we could see some of the rugs were saturated, and along the walls, there was standing water. We had a sump pump pit in the basement, but in the five years we'd lived there, we never experienced any water troubles; so we didn't put in a pump. Thankfully, Nathan's parents who lived across the street had one handy so he ran over to get it. In a matter of minutes, the pump was installed and operating. Then, we began rolling up and hauling out carpet to dry on the driveway, and piling up toys in the center of the room where the water hadn't yet reached. We worked all day long and into the night. But when the spring rains eased up, water still continued to leak into our basement. Eventually, we had a need for a second sump pump to work simultaneously with the first one, just to keep up. A few times, Nathan stayed awake all night to keep an eye on the water levels in the sump pump pits. Sometimes, we used a shop vacuum along the walls if our two pumps weren't fast enough. The water continued to pour in by the gallons! I measured for every four to five minutes, approximately seven gallons was kicked out through sump pump hoses. This continued for weeks. We speculated that there was an underground spring because we also had standing water in the yard near the house. I wish I could have bottled some of that water and repurposed it somehow. Laundry perhaps? Bathwater for the boys? Or washing dishes maybe? I probably could have filled a large swimming pool with it at the very least. A section of our front yard did stay pretty green throughout the summer as the hoses sent out a steady stream of water onto the lawn.

As if we weren't wading through enough troubles (pun intended), about the same time I began noticing some unusually fast crawling bugs throughout our house. Not a lot; just one or two at first, down in the basement. But then, I saw one on the main level and even another in our master bathroom on the second story. With the next one caught, I decided to study it briefly before squashing and flushing. I'm not afraid of insects, but I have a strict not-in-my-house policy! I went on my computer to try and identify it, although I had a sneaking suspicion of what it was; and prayed I was wrong. Unfortunately, *Google Images* was spot on with a match. We had cockroaches! I thought only places like New York City dealt with these kinds of nuisances, but apparently, Wisconsin had them too and they relished the damp conditions our wet basement offered. This was disturbing, to say the least, and I felt nauseous at the realization. What disheartened me most was learning that these pests produced allergens that aggravated asthma and other respiratory diseases. Discovering this, I felt so utterly defeated. How was I ever going to keep a sanitary, antibacterial, hypoallergenic home for my family, and my boys especially? I felt like such a failure. But of course, I couldn't curl up in a fetal position and cry. I had water to suck up and insects to exterminate. I shut my laptop, breathed a prayer asking God to give me perseverance, and then I told the kids I was headed to the hardware store for some roach poison- and maybe some French lavender scented Calgon bubble bath for myself if they had it in stock. *Calgon, take me away!*

When it rains, it pours, and a few days later, we had ourselves a storm. Normally, I love a good old thunder storm but after our troubles with water, I cringed at any sign of precipitation. This particular afternoon storm happened to bring some serious lightning and suddenly, we were without power. I was home alone with the kids when everything fell silent; the TV, the familiar hum of the fridge, and of course all the lights. I casually said to the kids,

"Well, we'd better go find some candles." But as the eerie stillness settled in, I soon realized we had a much bigger problem than a dark house with no TV. The sump pumps were no longer working! I jumped from the couch to my feet immediately.

"Oh no! The basement!" Without electricity, our sump pumps quit working, which meant our basement was filling up with water once again.

"Kids, find some ice cream buckets while I run outside and get the garden hoses!" We were going to have to do this the old fashioned way and somehow keep the water from pouring in. I ran out into the storm and grabbed two hoses from our back yard and hauled them through our house, down to the basement. I tried not to think about them being covered in mud and grass as I frantically dragged them across sections of carpet and down the stairs. The basement was pitch black. We only had one small window well to offer any kind of natural light down there so I sent the kids back upstairs to search out every single candle and flashlight in the house. Meanwhile, I started connecting and stretching hoses by the light of my cell phone. The trouble was, they still weren't long enough to reach from the sump pump pit to Carson's downstairs bedroom window well. I needed more length! I ran back outside to our neighbor's house and borrowed another long hose. By this time, I was soaking wet, muddy, out of breath, and feeling very panicky. Water was spilling onto the basement floor as I tried to show the kids how to fill buckets of water from the sump pump pits. Then carefully, so as not to spill, they carried the buckets to Carson's bedroom window well and poured the water outside. Meanwhile, I frantically tried to connect hoses, get a syphon started and send the water out of the house. I finally got a flow of water going through the hoses and then I took a moment to text Nathan and let him know what was going on.

"Help! Power went out at home and we are bailing the basement with buckets and hoses!" Nathan wasn't working too far away and within minutes he was able to come home and give the kids and me a hand with the buckets. Then, about twenty minutes later, we saw the light at the end of our dark tunnel, literally. We had power again!

Once, I was given advice from a friend to take one day at a time. But on occasion, I've found it necessary to take one moment at a time. This was one of those times. It was a marvelous moment when the power came back on and we heard the sound of the sump pumps take over our job of hauling ice cream pails of water by hand. All five of us collapsed to the floor with relief. But the moment quickly faded for me as I realized I was covered in grass, mud and drenched from the rain. I looked around at my smelly, damp basement with rolled up carpet and giant piles of toys, kid's costumes, muddy hoses, dripping buckets, and shop vacuums. I felt like tossing it all in a giant dumpster. And if I was really honest, I was tired of fighting for my house. I was getting to the point where I was almost too worn-out to care. From the lice and roaches, to the germs, flooding and the mess it left behind; I was done!

"Lord, we are ready for the second coming. Seriously! Come

Lord Jesus!" As I watched Nathan struggle, I knew he was probably ready too. The whole basement affair felt like it was the straw that broke the camel's back. With all of our trials over the past year it seemed as if this was our family's version of the Biblical plagues of Egypt. Later that evening Nathan and I tried to make some sense of our downstairs mess and I attempted to make light of the situation.

"Let's see, we've experienced tick-borne diseases which landed me in the hospital for a week, two life-threatening diagnoses, and depression all around, a lice infestation, cockroaches, and a flooded basement lasting a month. What's next, boils?"

Nathan didn't think my stab at stand-up comedy was funny. He gave me a glare that said, "Don't even go there." However it was Anders' optimistic attitude that gave us the break in the clouds we needed. He came bounding down the stairs breathless.

"Mom! Dad! I just had a great idea! If we let the basement fill up with water, then we'd have a place for a pet dolphin to live." His sincere belief that Make-A-Wish would actually grant him a pet dolphin to live in our home was just about the cutest thing ever and I wanted to savor the moment in the midst of our stinky, wet, disaster of a basement forever. I pulled Anders into a big hug as we sat on the cement floor. For a brief minute, I let him believe in the possibility. Then, I explained about salty ocean water and how much dolphins loved to jump and play and have plenty of room to swim. He began to look around our confining basement and understood. I kissed his head and thanked God for the gift of an innocent child.

A few days later, Nathan and I found ourselves continuing to stress over the basement predicament. I decided however, that it was time to boost morale within our family and tentatively approached Nathan with an idea. It was only early June, but the next day's forecast was looking lovely with summer-like temperatures near eighty degrees.

"I was thinking that since tomorrow is supposed to be really warm outside, we could all take a short break from the house; *if* the water level in the basement allows. I heard Sand Lake Beach is nice right now and I know the kids would love to go swimming. Even if it's just for a little while. We could pretend that everything is fine and we don't have any problems or stress or anything. What do you think?" Nathan didn't take long to answer.

"It's a great idea and I think you and the kids should definitely go." I caught his meaning; he was going to stay back and work. I understood his strong sense of obligation and the need to care and provide for us. But I felt the same, with a responsibility to keep spirits up in the family. An hour at the beach seemed like an important priority to me. So the next morning, I told the kids about my plan to spend a short time at Sand Lake during lunch. There was a cheer from all three. Everyone agreed to pitch in and help with some house cleaning first and then I packed a picnic basket with sandwiches, chips, grapes, and some drinks. A few hours later, the kids and I were in the van heading to the beach, free from the gloomy wet basement!

When we arrived, I was surprised at how quiet it was at the beach, with only two other families there and a few geese and goslings further down the lake. I spread out our things on the sand, sprayed my three impatient kids down with sunscreen and sent them off to swim. It didn't take long and they were fitted with snorkel gear, searching for snails, doing handstands in the lake and jumping off the dock. I captured an awesome photograph of all three of them taking a giant leap off the end together. It felt so good to be outside, away from the house, and laughing with the kids. Like a real summer day. I took a deep breath and enjoyed every second of it.

Time ticked away all too quickly though. I looked at my watch realizing we would soon need to pack up and head home. Nathan would want me to get back soon, to shop vacuum a corner area of the basement that caused trouble if we ignored it for too long. We ate our picnic lunch, and the kids were able to swim a few minutes longer. Then, we gathered our belongings and left the beach. It was not too long in the van when Carson made first mention of a new problem.

"Mom, I'm feeling really itchy. Can I take a shower when we get home?" I automatically guessed something was wrong when my now twelve-year-old son volunteered to take a shower. Normally it was like pulling teeth to get that kid to bathe. Then Anders chimed in.

"Yeah, I'm itchy too Mom. You got any lotion?"

By the time we pulled into our driveway, all three of the kids were complaining and wiggling in their seats. My mind went to the possibility of what my parents used to call "chiggers." They spoke of getting this after swimming in lakes when they were kids, although, I really didn't know what it all entailed. I had the kids show me their arms and legs but didn't see any sort of rash or bite. I told them all to take showers while I went to my laptop to research my trusty symptom-checker websites. As I did some reading on swimmer's itch, I realized that the *signs* of Canadian geese we saw that day within areas of Sand Lake Beach, coupled with the snails my kids collected, were the perfect recipe for them to be itching and scratching from certain parasites in the water. And the peppering of spots and welts that showed up all over their bodies the next morning was proof that they did indeed have the dreaded swimmer's itch. My joke to Nathan about the Biblical plagues wasn't too far off after all! I texted my husband that we'd been hit with more pestilence.

"Plague 7 has arrived: boils indeed!"

Within a minute Nathan called from work and I described to him over the phone what I was seeing.

"The boys are covered evenly in a sprinkling of tiny, red, itchy, dots. They are everywhere; on their arms, legs, stomach, face, and back. Ella on the other hand, appears to have a worse reaction. Her spots are more like quarter-sized welts all over her body. She looks … well … she looks …" I was at a loss for words with Ella standing there wearing the most pathetic, miserable look on her face. But Anders completed my sentence with childlike honesty, loud enough for Nathan to hear over the phone.

"She looks *really bad* Dad!" And with that bit of truth, I couldn't help it. In an effort to stifle a chuckle, I let out a giant snort instead. But it was no use as complete belly laughter soon followed. Of course, the boys joined in along with some finger pointing at their poor sister, which in turn made Ella burst into sobs. She stomped into her room in dramatic fashion and finished with a loud door-slam. I quickly told Nathan I needed to hang up and rectify the situation. Then, bringing all three of my kids into the bathroom I turned their faces toward the mirror and showed them just how pathetic all three of them appeared. The boys had no idea their faces looked like a Valentine sprinkled cupcake! Ella began to feel better when she saw that Anders even had spots where the sun didn't shine. Soon, they were all pointing and laughing, itchy and miserable together.

It was incredibly important to me that I find ways to laugh. Otherwise we might cry all the time!

> Proverbs 17:22, *"A cheerful heart is good medicine, but a broken spirit saps a person's strength."*

With all of our troubles, I knew that our strength would be fading fast if we didn't find some cheer soon. Laughter was essential. The book of Ecclesiastes talks about there being *"a time for tears and a time for laughter."* When you can know for sure that this world and all its problems are only temporary, then it is possible to step away from whatever circumstance is "bugging" you (e.g. lice, ticks, roaches, chiggers) and somehow see the humor in it. Speaking from experience, a good hard laugh, so hard you snort, can make you feel better and give you a fresh perspective. With the promise of Calamine lotion, Children's Benadryl, and a heaping bowl of cookie dough ice cream, my kids' outlook continued to improve.

> 2 Corinthians 4:17, *"For our light and momentary troubles are achieving for us an eternal glory that far outweighs them all."*

Chapter 9

A BOATLOAD OF JOY

Even though it had only been a couple of months, it felt like forever since we had heard an update from the Make-A-Wish Foundation. Nathan and I happened to be driving alone in the van one day when I received a phone call from a staff person named Janice at Make-A-Wish Wisconsin. She couldn't wait to give us incredible news.

"Leanne, I'm calling because the board of trustees met this past week and made the decision to revise their policy against granting motorized vehicles. The new guidelines will now allow wish-kids to receive certain motorized equipment as long as the motor stays within a certain size or horsepower. Which means Carson is going to get his boat!" My jaw dropped as I realized what her words meant.

"They changed the rules for him?" I asked her to hold while I put the phone on speaker. "Can you say that again so my husband can hear you too?" As she went on to explain and then ask us about our opinions on what Carson's boat should include and the style that would suit him best, Nathan and I were absolutely giddy. Our boy was going to have his dream come true, what a gift! This would be such an unbelievable, happy, shock for Carson. We had tried to make him understand that receiving a boat from Make-A-Wish wasn't a sure thing, due to their existing policy. He probably thought it wasn't going to happen.

We came up with a plan to surprise Carson with his wish-granting party on Father's Day, which just so happened to be one week away. The party would be made extra special because Nathan's brother, Jared, his wife and their three kids from Wyoming had plans to visit us during that same time. I quickly created an invitation for those friends and family who were an important influence in our son's life. After all the difficult trials we had experienced over the last year, we wanted to share this joyful and exciting moment with as many people as possible. Finally, something to celebrate! I was somewhat vague in the invitation, saying:

You are invited to Carson's wish party! Shhhh ...

Help us SURPRISE Carson on Sunday, June 14th, 2014 (Father's Day) when he finds out that his wish has been granted. Please come promptly at 5:40 PM to our house. Carson will arrive at 6:00 PM, just in time for the Make-A-Wish Foundation to reveal his gift!

Supper provided.

Since it was Father's Day, it made sense to send Nathan, his dad Jon, Nathan's brother Jared, and our boys fishing for the afternoon. We lived only three miles from the St. Croix River and we often had success catching fish from shore. The plan was for them to wrap things up around 5:45 PM and pull up at our home at exactly 6:00 PM. Meanwhile, the surprise party guests would be on our front porch to greet Carson. I had a lot to do to prepare, but at the same time, I could hardly wait for the big day.

One of the items on my to-do list for the party was to communicate with our local press and invite them. Holly, from Make-A-Wish, had mentioned to me that if the media should contact us in regard to the story, to give them a specific statement written by the foundation. Receiving press was very common as wishes were being granted to terminally ill children and it was an important and necessary way for Make-A-Wish to obtain free advertising and promote the organization. In fact, they heavily relied on this type of outreach.

I looked forward to sharing this news story with our local newspapers. In the past year, they had featured our family several times as we dealt with the heart wrenching diagnosis of CF. Now that something positive and exciting was happening, I wanted to share an updated, feel-good story with our community. I also thought that with all Make-A-Wish was doing for our family, it was important to give them the recognition and press they deserved. With my employment at the literacy council, I often wrote press-releases, so I had several contacts from the papers. I sent them an email with the secret information and party details. Later, I decided to include a few local TV stations, because I felt like the evening news was too often filled with sad and depressing stories. Here was a much needed, positive story, full of sentiment, especially as it landed on Father's Day.

As the week went by, I heard from several of the papers and they definitely wanted to feature something about it. But it wasn't until the day before the party that I got a phone call from the Minneapolis, St. Paul NBC affiliate, KARE 11 news, asking if they could send a film crew to the house.

"Of course! I'd love to see Make-A-Wish receive the attention they deserve. You are very welcome to come." And I gave them the timeline for Sunday's events:

> **2:30 PM:** Nathan, Jon, Jared and the boys leave to go fishing on the St. Croix River.
>
> **2:35 PM:** Ella, the Stenberg girls and I begin cleaning and decorating our house and front porch. Also get food and beverages prepared for the surprise party.

5:00 PM: Mike and Holly, our wish-grantors will arrive with cake and be available for press interviews.

5:40 PM: Guests will arrive for the party and assemble on our front porch ready to surprise Carson.

6:00 PM: Nathan, Jon, Jared, and the boys arrive. We'll let the realization sink in for a few minutes that Carson is about to have his wish granted. He should figure it out when he sees Mike and Holly and the Make-A-Wish banners on the porch.

6:05 PM: Steve Stenberg will drive up with Carson's brand new Alumacraft boat hitched to his truck for the big reveal!

The reporter from KARE 11 said they'd probably arrive around 5:00 PM unless of course another, bigger story should happen to break at the same time. I could hardly contain my excitement! But somehow, I managed to keep the information that they were coming, from everyone, except Nathan and our neighbor Steve, who would be showing up with the boat.

At last, Father's Day arrived and everything about the day was going like clock-work. Even the weather cooperated, giving us blue skies and seventy degrees! But soon after lunch things changed when I received a phone call from yet another TV news reporter. This one was a FOX News affiliate, KMSP Channel 9. As he spoke I realized that he was in route at the time.

"Wait, did you say you're on your way to our house right now?" It was only 1:00 PM.

"Yes, we're probably about forty minutes away. We wondered if we could try to capture some footage of the boys while they fish. And then, stop by to film you and your friends decorating and getting ready for the party. Is that possible?"

I was taken aback, "Well, the goal was for all of this to be a huge surprise for Carson. He has no idea that any of this is happening."

The reporter continued, "Right. What if we try and stay undercover? And if we happen to encounter Carson, we could just tell him we're in the area shooting a piece on the St. Croix River, and ask if he would mind answering some questions about fishing. How does that sound?"

I was reluctant to agree. This sounded risky. We had tried so hard to keep this all a big secret from him. I quickly gathered my thoughts and suggested a plan to the reporter.

"The boys weren't planning to go fishing until later on. But what if I sent them now, and your crew came to our house first. You could film us getting ready for the party, do some interviews, and then if there's time, catch up with the fisherman down by the river and possibly capture some secret footage of them. Their fishing spot is only a few minutes away from our place."

"Great! I love it. We'll see you in about thirty minutes."

I hung up, fighting against panic mode. FOX News was literally on their way to our house! First, I needed to tell Nathan that our plans had changed and to get Carson out of the house as soon as possible. Once that was arranged, I took a deep breath and contemplated the situation which was about to descend on my house in a matter of minutes. Normally, I love hosting parties, but this had the potential to turn into a circus! Our guest list had reached about sixty people. Combine the element of surprise and the emotion of my son receiving a gift from Make-A-Wish and you get a giant boost of adrenaline! Now, add the fact that a TV news crew was set to arrive and film our family and friends for the next few hours as we prepared for the party. I was a little frantic!

As soon as Nathan and the boys left for fishing, I gathered Ella and our neighborhood friends for a huddle, and told them what was going to descend upon our home very soon. With wide eyes, they all got very excited and we worked together to straighten up the house, blow up balloons, bring out markers and poster paper, and take out the food preparations. In no time at all the kids notified me with their excited voices that the FOX 9 News truck had arrived.

"Here we go!" I said out loud as I walked to answer the front door and let the chaos begin. There stood a handsome reporter with whiter-than-white teeth, a slick-back hairstyle, wearing a trendy, lavender, button-up shirt with flashy tie, and white dress pants; probably to match his teeth. I thought to myself, *you must be from out of town.*

As filming and interviews began, I knew that this was yet another unique opportunity for our family to be a witness of our faith in God, through the good times and bad. And with that purpose and vision, I relaxed. Our afternoon progressed smoothly and I kept in touch with Nathan, letting him know about the flurry of activities taking place at our home. The news crew even made a successful quick drive to the river and captured some film of our boys fishing. Mike and Holly, along with the second news crew from NBC's KARE 11 showed up right on schedule; the excitement increased another notch with their arrival. Our guests began trickling in thirty minutes later, surprised by the unexpected TV cameras. Soon all we had left was to wait for the fishermen. I felt so much anticipation I thought I might burst! More than sixty people on my front porch and lawn, banners and balloons, TV crews, local newspaper reporters, and a brand new fishing boat, just a few blocks away, stood waiting for my son Carson to arrive. And then, I got a text from Nathan at 5:50 PM; just ten minutes before they were supposed to show up.

"Trying to leave but my dad has a fish on... It's big." My first thought was,

"Are you kidding me?" But with everything at stake, I knew that for Nathan to allow this, Jon must have a *monster* fish on the line. I laughed and told our guests and the news crews what was happening.

"So apparently the fishermen are fighting a *big one* and need to make us all wait a few extra minutes!" Thankfully everyone understood. Nathan texted again not long after with the following message:

"Still trying to land it." I wrote back somewhat aggravated,

"This had better be a trophy fish. Hurry up!!!!!" And then, a few seconds later I received a picture. In it were Nathan, Carson, and Jon standing near the riverbank holding up the biggest, fattest, ugliest carp I'd ever seen! It must have weighted at least twenty pounds. I showed our waiting guests the picture and they responded with equal excitement. The reporters, all very impressed, asked me to email them the photo so they could add it to their coverage. It made for the perfect story!

Finally, the moment arrived and I was suddenly overcome with emotion as I caught sight of Nathan's truck pulling up with Carson in the front seat. But as I looked around, I wasn't the only one with tears in my eyes. The neighborhood was absolutely electric with anticipation. About a dozen or more kids were jumping up and down in the cul-de-sac, and our guests on the porch and in the yard were clapping and cheering for Carson while the film crews captured it all. His face showed shock and joy mixed together. When he saw the familiar faces of Mike and Holly approach him, wearing their blue Make-A-Wish shirts, he knew *exactly* what this was all about. His familiar dimple came out and you couldn't wipe the smile from his face as he hugged Mike and Holly both.

"Well Carson, do you know why we're all here?" Holly asked with a playful tone of voice.

"Um ... yeah I think so!" he said, bewildered but excited. He looked around at all of his family and friends standing nearby and asked, "Is this my wish party?"

"It certainly is!" said Holly. "So are you ready to have your wish granted?"

"Yes!" answered Carson, without hesitation. The crowd responded with cheers and whistles. Then Holly placed a brand new blue life jacket around his neck and told him,

"Well, you're going to need *this* if you want to use it." Then we heard the sound of a large pick-up truck come driving through the cul-de-sac pulling a beautiful, brand new, shiny black Alumacraft Escape 165 with 25HP motor.

Carson, the moment he realized his wish was about to come true.

A sharp gasp came from Carson's mouth as he caught sight of it.

"Oh my word!" he said incredulously. "Is it a boat?!" His friends all surrounded him with cheers and pats on the back. And as the truck and trailer came to a halt in front of our house, Carson immediately walked over and reached out a hand to touch the side of the boat, allowing himself the belief that this might actually belong to him. Nathan stood right behind him doing the very same thing and when Carson realized it, he turned and gave his dad the biggest hug ever. Of course all the TV cameras were right in their faces, getting the emotional moment on film. My heart was full as I stood beside them in awe.

Later that night, when the guests had all gone home, and the food and cake were put away, the five of us went upstairs to watch the 10:00 PM news. It was surreal to see our family being featured. And to think that a gorgeous new boat which Carson proudly christened, "*First Wish*," was now sitting in our garage thanks to generous donors and the Make-A-Wish Foundation. Carson decided to sleep in his boat that night. I think it's safe to say this was the happiest day of our son's life. And in many ways, it was ours too. It wasn't long ago that Nathan and I had been witnesses to the very worst day of his life. As a parent, it was the most dreadful thing we had experienced. So to see his spirit completely reversed and uplifted. It was truly just as much a gift to us as it was to him.

Chapter 10

PINE BUTTE GUEST RANCH

Our basement woes began to dry up as the summer progressed. With a new fishing boat, we were all enjoying the season with relief. Carson earned his Boater's Safety certificate, and was gaining independence as a twelve-year-old boy by being able to drive friends and family in his very own boat. Although, it made me a bit uneasy to see him operating a high powered motor, okay, change that to *very* uneasy, I knew it was good for him to experience the freedom. To feel the wind on his face, escape his troubles, be in control of something, and have the opportunity to spend time doing what he loved so much. The boat was a powerful medicine.

Thanks to the kindness of Nathan's friend, Kenton, we had another gift to look forward to at the end of July: an incredible family vacation at the dude ranch. We were all counting the days for our trip to the Pine Butte Guest Ranch in Choteau, Montana. Our plan was to start out for the twenty hour drive on the morning of Saturday, July 26, 2014, and stop halfway for the night in Miles City, Montana. The kids traveled well in the van and through the generosity of a local church group, we were able to purchase a high-powered adapter for our vehicle which allowed the boys to plug in their airway clearance machine and nebulizer to complete their Vest therapy while driving in the van! What a convenient timesaver this was for our family to be able to accomplish these lengthy treatments as we drove.

Departure day arrived and with a strategically packed minivan, complete with cowboy boots, hats, and fly-fishing rods, we were ready for our western adventure. We woke up the kids at the B.C.D., (we call this the *butt-crack of dawn*), and after a quick trip to the restroom they headed straight to the van. I had them sleep in comfortable clothing so there was no need to change before climbing into the vehicle. Their seats were situated with pillows, blankets, things to do, water bottles, and breakfast items so we wouldn't have to stop for food. Away we went!

At the first sight of a hill somewhat resembling a mountain, Anders insisted I unpack his cowboy boots and hat for him to wear. As we got closer to this particular land form, he begged us to drive straight to it so he could climb it. This boy was excited!

"Trust us, Bubba, there will be much bigger mountains to climb when we get to the ranch and we promise to take you hiking in them." We talked with the kids about how this was going to be the trip of a lifetime. I wanted them to know that the ranch we were going to was a special place, one we could never afford. The rate for a week's vacation was *way* over our budget and we learned that even celebrities were known to retreat at the Pine Butte Guest Ranch. As I looked at their website, I also recognized that it wasn't necessarily the ideal place for young kids. The ranch catered more to folks who were seeking peace and tranquility, such as avid bird watchers, photographers, hikers and conservationists. Certainly, children were welcome. However, I did have concerns our three could possibly be the *only* children staying at the ranch that week. So we gave them fair warning that they might be hanging out with their siblings.

The drive was long, but as we put the miles behind us, anticipation only grew. During our second day of driving, we made a bit of a detour so we could stop and visit Nathan's friend Kenton and meet his family. They lived in Helena, Montana. It was very special to see these two childhood friends reunite and then introduce one another to their families. I could almost picture Nathan and Kenton as young boys again, picking up easily where they left off. Kenton was humble when I asked him to show us some of his photography. He had taken many unbelievable images of wildlife that had graced the pages of National Geographic and Nature Conservancy's Magazine and I wanted to see his work first hand. He was practically a celebrity in the wildlife photography world. Kenton was able to pull out a few of his favorites and tell us the amazing stories behind capturing them. And then, unexpectedly, he held out a large print displayed uniquely against a thick sheet of aluminum and said,

"Here, I want you guys to have this one." It was a stunning photograph of a colorful rainbow trout, swirling in the water. We were struck once again by Kenton's generosity and thoughtfulness.

"This is going up on our mantle in the living room." I told Nathan. And then I asked Kenton to autograph it. What a wonderful keepsake he gave us. Now, we would think of him and his precious family every time we looked at it. Carefully, we wrapped the artwork and stored it in the van so it wouldn't get damaged from the rest of our luggage. After saying goodbyes, our family climbed into our all-too familiar seats for the final 150 miles of the trip.

"Pine Butte Guest Ranch, here we come!"

It's usually the last part of a road trip that seems to take the very longest, and this was no exception. We were within the last sixty minutes of a twenty-two hour-long journey before reaching our destination. Of course, being in small-town Montana, that last hour of driving was all gravel roads. This wouldn't be a huge deal except when two of your passengers have really bad gas. You want the windows down to get a breath of fresh air but you can't because giant clouds of dust and rocks would enter the vehicle. Add in a lengthy, unexpected detour with vague road-signs, and you get some impatient, crabby passengers! The level of obnoxious and annoying behavior was at an all-time high and no amount of DVDs or electronics would work to keep the kids from whining, tattling, farting, asking, singing, announcing, poking, teasing, and torturing each other- and us. But finally- *finally* we saw a wonderful wooden sign telling us that Pine Butte Guest Ranch was just around the next bend! Soon, we were pulling into recognizable territory. It was familiar because we had seen pictures on their website, giving us a good idea of what the surroundings looked like. But photos, of course, never do justice to the true beauty. Sometimes, you have to experience it in person to fully understand and we were lucky enough to do so. I'll never forget the wonderful feeling of climbing out of our van and stepping foot onto the property for the first time. I inhaled a deep breath; and what I took in was the freshest, sweetest air I've ever smelled in my entire life. It was a mixture of pine, wildflowers, fresh cool water and a hint of grass and horses. The ranch was nestled in a valley surrounded by stunning mountains, jutting steep and majestic into the blue sky. The lower areas were covered in a green carpet of grass, flowers, and trees. We were all very much in awe. There were beautiful log cabins spread throughout the ranch property. A gorgeous main lodge was in the center, with a pretty front porch complete with sturdy rocking chairs to sit and enjoy the view. A young woman, who was the ranch hostess, came out to greet and let us know that the other guests were in the main dining hall having dinner. We were welcome to join them. We looked up toward the log building, with its beautiful wall of windows, and a boy appearing to be ten-years-old peeked out at us from inside. I nudged my kids and pointed up in the boy's direction. When Anders saw him his eyes lit up.

"Hey, there *are* other kids here," he said excitedly.

We had arrived at the ranch about an hour later than expected because of the detour. When the hostess told us of the delicious salmon and rice pilaf meal the guests were enjoying inside, we quickly regretted our on-the-road supper stop at Burger King. But our stomachs were disappointingly full so instead, she asked if we'd like to be shown to our home away from home for the next week and get settled. It turns out we didn't have to go far as our cabin was the closest one to the main dining hall. As we stepped inside, we were all absolutely delighted with the accommodations. The cabins were a perfect combination of rustic and plush. They went above and beyond our expectations with big, comfortable log beds for everyone, cozy couches and a gorgeous wood fireplace.

"I can't believe we get to be here!" I said out loud. That phrase continued to be said over and over again throughout the entire week as we were treated to the beauty and luxury of the Pine Butte Guest Ranch. What an honor and privilege to stay in such a place. We certainly didn't deserve it.

With the height of the mountains surrounding the ranch, sunset seemed to come early. But we still had a little bit of time to explore before turning in for the night. We all wanted to see the horses, check out the lodge and investigate a crystal clear mountain stream that ran right behind our cabin. That night I could hardly wait to fall asleep with my bedroom window open, so I could listen to the sounds of the babbling water from the pretty little stream and breathe in deep, the fresh mountain air. Who needed the *Mountain Stream Nature Sound CD* to help you fall asleep or an aerosol can of Glade Clear Spring air freshener to make your bathroom smell better when you had the real thing?

When it was too dark to see outside, we decided to call it a night and get ready for bed. We were completely wiped out from the long drive and it was only the beginning of our exciting vacation in the Montana Rocky Mountains. The boys were able to get their evening Vest treatments done in the van before arriving at the ranch, so bedtime routines consisted only of administering some medications, taking showers, brushing teeth and getting pajamas on. And then, without even prompting the kids, they all gathered onto the master bed for what became a sort of *Kum-ba-yah* moment. Everyone got quiet, contemplative and cuddly so I decided to take the opportunity for us all to spend a few moments in prayer; the family agreed. Nathan and the kids each took the chance to sincerely thank God for bringing us to this wonderful place. They thanked Him for creating the mountains, the horses, for giving us the chance to go fishing and make some new friends. When it was my turn, I felt a sudden inspiration to pray these things,

"Lord, I'm in awe that we get to be here in this beautiful place. Thank you. And I sense that you brought us here for a reason. I think it's more than just simply to enjoy a family vacation and your beautiful creation. While we're here, I pray that our family could be a witness for you, and an encouragement to the staff and other guests. Please use us. Amen." Unknowingly, we would see an incredible answer to that prayer just six days later.

The next morning was the start to our first full day at the ranch. Once the boys were done with their Vest therapy, we headed over to the main lodge for breakfast. This is where all of the guests ate their meals together. Not only was it a treat for me to not have to cook for an entire week, but the ranch hired gourmet chefs to prepare healthy but decadent meals for their guests. We were definitely spoiled. It was during this time that our family got a better glimpse of the twenty-five people we would be spending the week with. It appeared that several of the guests were retirees and a few were thirty-something. No kids were in the dining room yet. As we found a table to sit at, the screen door squeaked and in walked a boy and girl who appeared to be about the same age as Carson and Ella. Anders' eyes lit up and he whispered,

"Mom, there's that boy from last night!" They came over by our table along with their parents and it didn't take long for our two families to start talking. We learned that Joe and his wife Carla, and their two children, Giorgia and August, were from Colorado. Having kids can often times create a comradery, and allow for making friendships easier- this was no exception. It may sound overly spiritual but I had a feeling about this family. As the week progressed we got to know them better and for some reason I sensed we were going to make a unique connection with them that we'd never forget.

All that week, we went for horseback rides in the mountains, hiked to scenic glacier lakes and waterfalls, had cookouts beneath

incredible jutting buttes and explored and fished in crystal streams
with this family. We stayed up late to star gaze and tell stories. We
swam in the heated pool and watched the sunset over Indianhead
Mountain. The girls brushed and braided the horses' tails and manes
while the boys built dams in the stream and fished Cutthroat Trout
for hours. A blue grass band entertained us one evening in the
lodge. My favorite song they performed was an old hymn, *"I'll Fly
Away."* These were all wonderful memories to treasure and hold in
our hearts forever.

If there's one thing I've learned with our boys being diagnosed
with a life-threatening illness, it's to remember that our time on
earth is fleeting, and we should live each day with no regrets. Playing
with our kids, saying meaningful words to others, and taking time
to make someone smile is more important than earning money and
living for our own gain. At the end of our life we won't long for more
time at the office. But we might wish we had forgiven more quickly,
said "I love you" more often, and spent time just listening to people.
The CF diagnosis changed my thinking and forced me to lighten
my work load and put my family first, as it should be. So during
our vacation especially, I enjoyed simple activities such as sitting on
the front porch of the main lodge while watching the sun set. One
night I did so with one of the ranch's volunteer staff members, an
older gentleman named Dan Imming.

**Dan Imming, PBGR volunteer. Photo taken
just days before the accident.**

We chatted about life and family and I learned that he and his wife, Susan, were from Colorado. She usually accompanied him to Pine Butte but stayed back this time while he volunteered at the ranch for several weeks. As we talked, hummingbirds buzzed back and forth in front of us sipping sugar water from feeders while the sun slipped over a spectacular backdrop of mountains. My kids and their friends were oblivious to the splendid scenery as they laughed and raced mountain bikes around the ranch yard. It was an absolutely perfect evening and I tucked it away in the scrapbook of my mind. Little did I know, that memory would become priceless in just a few short days.

Chapter 11

THE ACCIDENT

July 31, 2014: As was routine during our stay at the Pine Butte Guest Ranch, the vacationers ate evening meal together in the dining hall. Many of us had just come back from an exhilarating all-day hike, guided by Pine Butte staff members, Larry and Dan. They led us to Our Lake, a beautiful glacier lake. It was no simple task to get there but well worth the journey. Carson and I even had a close encounter with a family of mountain goats. I was able to sneak some amazing close-up photographs as they showed no fear, coming within a couple feet from us! At one point, we were ready to jump in the ice-cold lake if those big white goats took one step closer. Thankfully, a swim wasn't necessary.

The entire day was a literal mountain top experience and we all agreed it was one of the best days we'd ever had. Later that evening, feeling stuffed from a delicious dinner and dessert in the dining hall, we listened to announcements from the ranch director about the next day's activities being offered. First thing in the morning, there was to be a horseback ride to a lovely breakfast cookout. And in the afternoon, we were given the option to bring a sack lunch and take a tour of a neighboring cattle ranch, or visit a dinosaur museum. I signed myself, Ella, and Anders up for the cattle ranch tour. Carla and Giorgia decided to join us, while Nathan, Carson, and our friends, Joe and August, decided to go out on their own for another all day hike back to Our Lake.

The next morning, I set my alarm early, not only so I would be up and ready for the horseback ride, but also because I'd been meaning to capture a picture of a sunrise. I peeked out my bedroom window and sure enough, Indianhead Mountain gave off a magnificent orange glow from the reflection of the rising sun. Even though it was July, the mornings were always cool up in the mountains. I ran outside in the shorts and T-shirt I had slept in, complete with bedhead, and tiptoed barefoot in the cold, dewy grass. I figured most people would just be waking up and wouldn't notice me, but as I began snapping pictures with my phone, I was startled by Dan who happened to be walking by, handling some ranch chores.

"Good morning! You're up nice and early. It's a little chilly out here you know." Dan chuckled as he gave a cheerful greeting.

"Yes, it is." I said self-consciously, looking down at my shorts and bare feet. I stopped taking pictures and quickly ran back inside our cabin for cover.

A little bit later, with proper clothing attire, make-up on and hair brushed, I was ready for the horseback ride to the breakfast cook out. Ella came along too and the group of about ten riders wound our way along picturesque mountain trails with impressive scenic backdrops. It was like riding through a post card. The landscape of wild flowers along the hillside was in full bloom. The Indian paintbrush, liatris, rhododendron, columbine, phlox, elephant-head, and loosestrife were prettier than my own perennial garden back home. I marveled at the varieties and brilliant colors. God certainly was the Master Gardener. We finally reached a campsite where the smell of frying bacon and blueberry pancakes lured us in. Fresh coffee was brewing over the fire and once we dismounted our horses, the ranch staff served us up a hot and delicious breakfast around the campfire. It was the perfect morning.

A few hours later, it was time for the next set of adventures. Nathan and Carson, along with friends Joe and his son August, headed out for their all-day hike to Our Lake to do some fishing. Meanwhile, Anders, Ella, and I along with Carla and Giorgia, joined the other fifteen-or-so guests who also signed up for the cattle ranch tour which was about thirty miles away. Enough people had signed up that two vehicles were needed to take us all. Ranch staff members Larry and Dan were to be our drivers and with carefully packed lunches, we climbed into the ranch's white shuttle-vans. Ella hopped into one of the vehicles with Carla and Giorgia which was a Ford fifteen-passenger van driven by Larry. Anders decided to ride in the other vehicle; a Mercedes's Sprinter passenger van, similar to an airport shuttle or a FedEx truck. I followed to keep him in line. I instructed him to sit in the very back row because all of the other passengers in our van were in their seventies and eighties. I didn't think any of them needed to be maneuvering themselves uncomfortably into the back seat. Anders suddenly changed his mind about wanting to ride in this particular van, but I insisted that we were now situated in our seats and we were all going to the same place.

"Sorry, we're not going to switch vehicles now," I said. As far as I know, none of the passengers, including me and Anders buckled our seat belts, except the driver. I guess we all had a vacation-mode mentality, assuming that nothing bad could happen. The engines started and our two vans rumbled down the dusty road.

A rule of thumb, when driving on gravel roads, is not to follow too closely behind the vehicle in front of you. They can kick up a lot of dust and small rocks, easily putting a crack in your windshield. So our van stayed a safe distance behind the first. I sat in the middle of the very back seat while Anders was on my left and an older woman was seated on my right. I decided to take out my phone and spend some time looking through photos I had taken so far on our trip. I was showing them to the woman next to me and she marveled at how close I had gotten to the mountain goats during our hike yesterday. I was just about to show her a picture of Anders and August braving the icy waters of Our Lake when all of a sudden I felt our van veering off to the left. I looked up from my phone to see a passenger near the front, leaning forward with his arms up, and shouting at the driver.

"Whoa! Whoa! Whoa!" he said, repeatedly. There was no slowing down of the vehicle as we crossed the oncoming lane and then went down a steep ravine. Without warning, we were falling and rolling. I wasn't alarmed at this point but instead calmly thinking to myself, "So this is what it feels like to be in a rollover accident."

The sounds of breaking glass, rocks, bending steel, and people tumbling, groaning, filled the van. And then there was a splash. I certainly didn't expect to hear *that* sound. Finally, the vehicle came to a stop and there was silence. I opened my eyes to a thick cloud of dust within the van. It was hard to see my surroundings but I knew where I was and what had happened, never having lost consciousness. That is when the seriousness of the situation hit me and I immediately jumped into action.

My first thought was, "Dear God, where is my son?" and instantly, I heard a muffled and delirious cry from Anders. I felt around for him and found him only inches away, right at my feet. I scooped him into my arms and saw that the window near us was busted out. Thankfully, being the type of vehicle that it was, the windows were tall, making it easy to duck out and through them. Stepping down into what was a muddy creek; I carried my boy about ten feet from the vehicle and looked him over quickly. No broken bones. His face was a mess, most of which seemed to be caused by a bloody nose. I saw a few cuts on his head and lip, but other than that he seemed relatively okay, for now.

"Stay right here and do not move!" I instructed him. Then, I turned back to the van to assess the situation and the other passengers still inside. This is when I realized that our vehicle had flipped upside down, landing in the middle of a creek. What a scene! As I waded through the water, Anders called to me.

"Mama is this really happening or just a dream?" His question was absolutely relevant. One second we were driving along a gravel road, and now suddenly, our van was overturned and surrounded by water? I looked back in his direction.

"Yes Baby, this is really happening. So I need you to be the bravest boy ever. Can you do that for me?" I asked.

"Okay Mommy." He answered softly.

**The accident scene; Willow Creek along
Bellview Road, Choteau Montana.**

There wasn't time to say anything else to my precious boy. My quick assessment of the situation was that our van driver was trapped, upside down, buckled in his seat belt, and submerged underwater up to his waist! It was Dan! He wasn't moving. I waded to the driver's side door and tried with all of my strength to open it but with the pressure of the water, the muddy bank, and possibly a dent in the door, I wasn't strong enough to get it open. So I plunged my way through the water, around to the passenger door in an effort to reach him from the other side. All the while I kept thinking, "Dear God, help me! How much longer can this poor man go without breathing?" As I waded through the cold water I pushed floating debris out of my way: someone's sack lunch, a backpack, and a camera case. In all of my life I had never felt such alarm! My heart felt like it was going to beat out of my chest. I was living a scene from a chilling movie. However, the Lord allowed me to keep a clear presence of mind and not panic. Yes, I was terrified. But the fear did not once overtake me. I reached the passenger door, climbed through the broken window and grabbed for the seat belt, trying to unbuckle and set our driver free somehow. But it was no use. I soon made the assessment that Dan was gone. There was no movement, no struggle, or signs of life from him; only stillness. I regretfully left him there, realizing others were in distress and needed immediate attention.

Someone was calling out. It was the woman who had been sitting right next to me as we drove. I climbed out of the van and went to her.

"Ma'am! Are you alright?" I asked. She had made her own way out and was clutching her obviously injured wrist.

"Oh, I'm going to need surgery, I just know it. I'm going to need surgery." She kept repeating over and over again. I told her to sit down next to Anders as a second woman, still in the van, drew my attention. She appeared confused and injured, with broken facial bones and lacerations. She also had a probable broken arm and struggled to speak. I carried her out of the van and set her to stand outside of it. As she leaned on me for support, I steered her to the bank near Anders. She was a sight and I'm sure it frightened my son to see her injuries.

Next, was an elderly man, who was trapped among the seats in the center of the overturned van. Though he was eighty-six-years old, he showed the flexibility of a gymnast while pinned. He was facing upward and I'm sure the poor man was uncomfortable, but I was thankful to see him conscious, moving and even attempting to lift himself. My instinct was to help him out of there so I made my best effort to offer leverage, using all of my strength. I was able to get him into a more comfortable position but I could not carry him completely out of the van; after all, he was probably about 175 pounds and still wedged between the battered seats pretty well. I was disappointed that my adrenaline didn't lend more super-powers to the situation. He sort of chuckled at the predicament and I marveled at his positive attitude. Although, it struck me later that he may not have caught sight of Dan's condition, or anyone else's for that matter. I told him to rest and sit still for a few moments while I looked for others who needed help. There were more passengers to take into account and honestly, I hadn't even paid much attention to whom or how many were in our van when we left for the cattle ranch tour. Maybe eight or nine people total? I prayed I wouldn't find more passengers like our driver.

As I continued my evaluation of the situation, I saw two more men in their seventies who were still inside the van, hopelessly working to rescue Dan. I could tell it was futile, not only because our driver had already passed away, but because the two men had obvious injuries of their own preventing them from making real progress.

"Guys, he's gone. You can stop now." I told them. But they kept working, pointless as it was. I respected them for trying.

It was at this time I realized we needed real professional help. I looked at our surroundings. Our van had tumbled about fifteen feet down a steep embankment and from the road, no one would ever be able to see us down there. So I climbed up to get a better view. The bank was full of thick brush and thorns which cut and tore at my legs. In the moment, I never felt or even noticed the deep slashes that would later leave permanent scars. Once at the top of the hill I was disheartened to see that we were in the middle of nowhere. No vehicles or much of anything were in sight except wide open plain with a backdrop of the beautiful mountains. My cell phone was gone, probably somewhere in the bottom of the creek; although it didn't really matter because out here there was absolutely no service. I ran back down the embankment through the brush and grabbed Anders.

"Bubba, I need your help and I want you to come up with me." I carried him through the brush to the top of the road and instructed him.

"Here is what I need you to do. Watch for cars or trucks and if you see one, I need you to jump up and down and wave your arms and yell as loud as you can for help, okay? We need to get someone's attention. Can you do that for us?" He nodded with understanding and I left him there so I could tend to the injured passengers once again.

There were the two women sitting on the muddy bank, the elderly gentleman still stuck in the van waiting patiently, and by this time, the other two men had made their way out, bewildered and now feeling the pain of their injuries. One had a serious laceration on his leg and I knew he needed medical attention right away. He seemed to be going into shock. The other man, who happened to be a physician, seemed to be in a daze and wasn't communicating much with anyone. His wife, who had been seated next to me at the time of the accident, seemed to think he may have hit his head.

It was unreal, the entire devastating scene. Everything seemed to be happening rapidly and yet in slow-motion at the same time. So many things were taking place at once. I noticed out of the corner of my eye, an overturned boot floating in the muddy creek. Not being completely sure if there were other victims unaccounted for, I waded back into the waist-deep water to see if someone else needed rescuing. I remember reaching out for the boot, praying to God that there wasn't a body attached to it. Thankfully, it came up as just an empty boot and I threw it up on shore with gratitude. I also pulled out a few other items; someone's water bottle, and a camp chair that had been tossed from the back of the van.

And that's when it hit me. Help wasn't coming fast enough. I trudged out of the water and looked at our pathetic situation. Time was ticking away as everyone was in pain, their injuries swelling, bleeding, and people going into shock, fearing for their lives. How long had it been since the accident? Five minutes? Ten? I climbed back up the ditch and stood beside Anders. Sheltering my eyes from the intense summer sun, I looked out across the vast country, oblivious to its beauty, and looked for any sign of a human presence.

Where are we anyway? I wondered. Having made an almost complete circle, I finally spotted a ranch that looked to be about a mile away.

"That's where I'm going." I said out loud. I turned down toward the van wreck and shouted to the victims.

"Okay guys, I'm going for help. I'll be back as soon as I can."

"You can't do that. You haven't got any shoes on!" One of the women stated. I glanced at my feet realizing she was right. My sandals must have been thrown off during the impact of the crash and I never even knew it until just now. But that fact didn't discourage my determination at all as I gazed down the rocky gravel road toward the lone ranch house. I had to go.

"I'll be fine." I reassured her. And then I told my son,

"Anders, I'll be right back. You stay here and watch for cars okay?"

"No Mommy, don't go!" He protested only once. But as I turned to leave I knew I was doing what needed to be done, for his sake as well as the rest of the group.

"I'll come back, Bubba. I promise!" I said to him over my shoulder as I started off down the long gravel road. I took about fifteen steps and then gave one last look in his direction. He appeared so pathetic, his face a mess, standing there seemingly alone. The van wreck and other passengers were completely out of view. During this time, no one comforted my little boy; the other passengers were all rightfully absorbed in their injuries. And yet miraculously Anders kept his composure. I'm not sure I could have done what was necessary if my son had been more upset. He did exactly what I told him to do, watching for cars along the side of the road while I ran for help.

"Dear God, be with my baby boy." I prayed. And then I couldn't look back again. Later, through counseling Anders revealed it was in that moment, "When you ran down the road Mama, that's when I prayed."

I realized very quickly that this type of gravel was much different than any kind I was accustomed to back home. These rocks were jagged, plentiful, and unforgiving as they tore through my bare feet. It would later take weeks to pull out all of the embedded rocks in them. I tried finding softer patches or ruts that might be easier to land on but there really wasn't any. I glanced along the ditches and considered running through those instead but they were filled with thick, dry, prickly looking bushes and I figured my legs would probably get torn up worse than my feet. The possibility of lurking rattlesnakes also kept me on the visible road.

As I ran, I had some time to process a few things. After trying to account for injured passengers from the crash I was finally given a moment to realize I might possibly be injured myself. My neck and jaw were sore and so were both of my forearms. I also felt some stinging on my legs and glanced down to see that they would require some medical attention. I had barely started running and I was already gasping for breath. Partly because of my shock, and partly because I had just been tossed about, then spent the last twenty minutes physically exerting myself by carrying, wading, lifting, pulling and climbing. It was also about 2:00 PM in the afternoon and a scorching ninety degrees; not exactly ideal conditions for a jog. Plus I was soaking wet, trembling and absolutely terrified; but I was not overcome by it. Because I recognized I was not alone; even on this remote Montana road. Every single, painful step of the way I knew that the Lord was with me. I may not have had the adrenaline rush I was hoping for when I tried to help Dan out of the van just minutes ago. But as I ran, I felt God carrying me closer toward the ranch house. There was a moment when I had to slow to a walk because I was so weary I thought I might trip and fall. I was disappointed in myself for doing so, but then a Bible verse suddenly came to mind.

Isaiah 40:30-31, *"Even youths grow tired and weary
and young men stumble and fall, but those who hope
in the Lord will renew their strength. They will soar on
wings like eagles. They will run and not grow weary.
They will walk and not grow faint."*

I kept my gaze up toward the house the entire time and it
eventually drew closer. I strained to see movement or some sort of
life in the yard and saved my voice for the very moment when I did.
And then, I noticed a flash of color near a shed. Could it be? Or
was my mind playing tricks on me? I stared hard in that one spot to
determine if it was a person. Maybe it was only an animal? Or just
something blowing in the wind? I began to run again so as to get
nearer and see better. As I got closer, approaching the entrance to
their driveway, I became more confident that what I saw was indeed
a person. I ventured to use my voice and test its certainty.

"Hey! Hey! I need help!" I yelled at the top of my lungs. And
the movement I saw in the yard responded by suddenly stopping.
To me, this confirmed that the person could hear me as they reacted
to my screams. With some relief I picked up speed and yelled more.

"Help! Please help!" The person appeared to be a boy of about
13 or 14, and later I learned his name was Garret. But the funny
thing was he ran not toward me but instead away. Soon it was
apparent why as he hopped onto a four-wheeler and started the
engine, whipping it around in the direction of the driveway and
eventually to me.

"Oh! What a smart kid!" I thought to myself. He quickly met
me at their mailbox and I was able to spit out the most crucial words
to him in between deep inhales and exhales.

"There's been a terrible accident and I need to call 911!" He had
me hop on the back of his ATV and we drove right to the front
door of his house. Together we burst into the living room where his
family was sitting together watching TV. I'm sure it was frightening

for them to have a strange woman come barging into their home unexpectedly. I was out of breath, wet, muddy, bloody, and frantic.

"Help! I need a phone to call 911! There's been an accident! Our van is upside down in the water and people are still stuck inside!" I was referring to the driver, the elderly man and possibly even others unaccounted for. My entrance caused immediate hysteria in the room as Garret's little sister began to scream and flee. His father, Lane, jumped up from the recliner, asking me where exactly the van was. He threw on a shirt and within seconds was out the door and on a vehicle, headed toward the crash scene. I later learned that when he reached the van, he plunged into the water and was able to free our driver from his seat thanks to incredible strength and a pocket knife. But it was too late; Dan had, of course, already passed.

As I stood in the doorway, Garret came to me with a phone and a panicky look on his face.

"It's not working!" he said. I realized that he may have been understandably flustered and I asked him to let me try. I put the phone to my ear and hearing no dial tone I shut the phone off, waited a second and then turned it back on. Dial tone! I entered 9-1-1 and waited for the ring. Finally, a dispatcher answered. I remember taking a deep breath and trying to explain, as calmly as I could, the events that had taken place.

"My name is Leanne and my family and I are vacationing at the Pine Butte Guest Ranch in Choteau. Our van was in a rollover accident and landed upside down in a creek about twenty miles from the ranch. I'm pretty sure there is at least one fatality." She asked me how many people were involved and I guessed about eight passengers, including my seven-year-old son. When questioned about our exact location, I handed the phone over to Garret's mom, Bev, because I really had no idea where we were. Once the call was completed, Garret, his mom, and his older sister took me back to the scene. I was anxious to return to Anders and continue helping the passengers. What a relief to know that real help was on the way! However, I was disheartened to discover that the closest hospital was forty miles from us. It was going to be a while before paramedics showed up at the scene.

When I got back to the site, my boy was still standing in the road, right where I left him and we met in a relieved hug. As I held him close, I thanked God for sparing his precious life because I knew there could have been a much worse outcome.

"See Bubba, I told you I'd come right back. You did such a good job while I was gone. I'm so proud of you." I found out later that Anders had taken it upon himself to offer some comfort to the other victims as they waited for help to arrive. He found breath mints in his pocket and walked around sharing them with people at the scene. It was a simple gesture and yet it absolutely amazed me that a young child could somehow set aside his own justifiable fears, think of others, and make an effort to cheer them. This small act spoke volumes to me.

Upon returning, I looked around and it appeared that a few neighboring ranch hands who were also first responders had arrived. They heard the dispatch go out after my 911 call was made and were there to offer aide. Garret's mom and sisters asked me if they could take Anders back to their house and distract him from the awful scene.

"Anders, would you like to come with us and have a Popsicle? Maybe watch cartoons for a little while?" He seemed interested and I was comfortable with that. Getting him away from the chaotic scene made sense. Just as Anders was being led away, one of the first responders asked me to come down and check on the victims. He may not have realized that I was actually one of them too but it didn't matter; I still had plenty of adrenaline coursing through me and I wanted nothing more than to continue helping. I ran down the embankment to see how everyone was doing. They were all out of the van by now and sitting in a huddle along the muddy bank. When the accident happened, we were on our way to a cattle ranch and our van was loaded with several camp chairs, two large jugs of lemonade and sack lunches for everyone. The day was to be pleasant as our group of vacationers planned to relax in the chairs under a shade tree, drink lemonade and learn about life as a cattle rancher. Now, those camp chairs were tossed all over the accident scene, some sunk in the creek. The idea came to set up the chairs and get the passengers a bit more comfortable as we waited for ambulances. I got to work immediately.

A man's leg was swelling up really badly and even in the ninety degree heat he was shivering. I worried about signs of shock. He was agitated and in a lot of pain.

"Come sit down here and try to stay calm." I pleaded. Then I noticed Garret's mom standing along the edge of the road holding blankets and water bottles. She had thoughtfully returned with them, thinking they might be of good use. I approached her at the top and took them from her with gratitude.

"Thank you so much! This is exactly what we needed." Then I carried everything down and immediately wrapped a blanket around the man. His wife was another one I worried about. She too was trembling and I could tell her face had broken bones as well as her arm. Her hair was matted and I was concerned about a possible head trauma too. She wasn't saying much at all. I brought her a water bottle and tried giving her something to drink. Mostly I just sat with her and gently rubbed her back to keep her calm. There wasn't much more I could do except wait with them. The elderly gentleman, the one who was stuck inside the van like a pretzel, now sat quietly in a camp chair with his feet dangling in the muddy water.

As I surveyed our pathetic situation, I questioned as Anders did, if this was really happening or just a dream? But then strangely, a feeling of comfort washed over me even as I looked at our overturned vehicle sitting in the water. In spite of the enormous tragedy before us I knew without a doubt that things could have been so much worse. And honestly the only emotions I felt at that moment were indescribable gratitude and relief! I decided to voice this to our group as we huddled on the muddy bank waiting for help to arrive.

"Guys, I know this sounds crazy, but I believe we have a lot to be thankful for right now. Do you mind if I pray?" There were no objections and a few of the victims readily bowed their heads. And then I began an audible conversation with the Lord right there.

"Dear God, even though we are really scared and hurting right now, we want to thank you for being with us. You protected and spared those of us sitting here and we are grateful. You have never left our side. Thank you that help is on the way."

As I prayed, I happened to be watching one of the victim's reactions and he was nodding his head in agreement and even saying "Yes." But then I saw something change in his facial expression as he looked over at Dan's lifeless body. He even began to shake his head no. I continued praying and asking God to comfort us and give us peace as we waited. But he just stared at Dan and his face grew cold with seeming resentment.

After my prayer I glanced out at the creek and something caught my eye. It was one of my missing black sandals floating in the muddy water along the other side of the bank. Determined to retrieve it, I waded over and leaned out as far as I dared but ended up sinking into a deep, mucky spot, falling in the creek up to my chest in the attempt. I did manage to get my sandal but decided that searching for the other one wasn't worth the effort so I humbly waded back to shore completely drenched. But I hung onto that sandal like an earned trophy.

Looking up toward the road I saw that more responders had arrived along with police. It was such a relief to *finally* see flashing lights even if it wasn't an ambulance. I called their attention to our little group down below.

"These people need help." With a pleading look, I pointed to the victim that gave me the most concern. It was then that I noticed Garret's sister standing along the road with Anders. She waved to me and I realized I was no longer needed as the rescuer of these people. It was time to focus all of my attention and energy on my boy. After all, he was a victim too. So I left my little group and climbed back up the bank for the last time.

"He just kept asking for you so we brought him back here. We cleaned up his face and gave him a Popsicle in an effort to take down the swelling. He has a laceration on the back of his head and he bit through his bottom lip." Anders interrupted her.

"Mommy, I got to have *two Popsicles*; a lime-green one and a grape one. And they let me watch cartoons too." Later, *The Great Falls Tribune* ran several articles about the accident. In one of them, written by David Murray, from August 9, 2014, Garret was quoted as saying, "He's the toughest little kid I've ever met."

I embraced Anders and thanked the teenage girl and her mom for taking such good care of him. Then, I looked for a place we could go that sheltered him from the crash site. He'd seen enough blood, injury, death, and wreckage to last a lifetime. We set up two camp chairs behind a parked police car on the road and Bev brought an iPad so Anders could watch a movie on it and hopefully become distracted. She even fetched me a pair of her daughter's flip flops so I wouldn't have to go barefoot any longer. They thought of everything! This family was such a blessing to us all. When I first saw their home in the distance, I knew they were my only option, but I had no idea they would be such angels, offering compassion and aid in countless ways. I learned a few days afterwards that if the accident had occurred just an hour later, this family would not have been home as they had plans to attend a rodeo in Bozeman which was three hours away. Praise God for this family!

With the arrival of the first ambulance on the scene, a huge weight was lifted from my shoulders. And then the realization of how exhausted I was, both physically and emotionally, hit me like a ton of bricks and I collapsed into the camp chair next to Anders. A second ambulance pulled up and the area became chaotic as more people were scurrying around, assessing the situation and offering medical attention to those who needed it. I mentioned to someone in passing that when there was time I'd like my son to be looked at, to make sure he was all right. An EMT stopped and knelt down next to Anders and then asked me if I was his mother. I told him yes and that we had both been in the accident. He waved over another paramedic and Anders and I were given an initial assessment. Looking back, I think first responders never even recognized that I was actually a victim in the accident because I was so involved in assisting at the scene. I didn't really come across as being injured. But once I was sitting and the realization of everything came crashing down I again began to notice my neck and jaw were pretty sore. I told the paramedics this and it caused a flurry of activity as one shouted for a cervical collar and another called for a stretcher.

"I don't think this is all necessary. I just ran a mile down this road for help and I've climbed up and down this embankment about six times!" I said with a chuckle.

"Just keep still ma'am, it's possible you could have broken vertebrae somehow. We're just following protocol so please remain calm," they explained. I worried that all of the new commotion suddenly surrounding us would frighten Anders. Just then we heard the sound of a helicopter and I tried distracting him with it.

"Hey Bubba, do you hear that? A helicopter is going to land in the field nearby. It's here to take some people to the hospital because it can travel much faster than an ambulance. Can you see it? Isn't that so awesome?"

An EMT informed me that Anders seemed to check out okay and all his vitals were normal.

"Thank you, Jesus." I said out loud. The paramedics helped me lie down on the stretcher and secure the C-collar around my neck. I didn't like being strapped down one bit because it limited my ability to properly observe what was happening around me. I could only hear voices and see the clear blue sky above me. It was at this time that anxiety and panic began to creep in. I kept calling to make sure Anders was nearby. I strained to hear who was around me and who was being taken where. I wanted to know how the other passengers were faring and if my husband had been notified yet.

"Has anyone contacted the Pine Butte Guest Ranch yet? The passengers from the van are all vacationing there and the ranch will want to know what's happened to us. Can someone please notify them? My husband's name is Nathan Waterworth," I begged.

It absolutely pained me to think about Nathan and Carson hearing the news of the crash and then wondering if Anders and I were alright. I also thought about Ella in the other van ahead of us. I'm sure she was questioning what happened to our group, having never arrived at the ranch tour like we were supposed to. I just wanted my family to know that Anders and I were safe and be spared of the awful worry and grief!

"Just stay calm ma'am. We're working on that right now," I was told. However this wasn't completely reassuring. It felt like an eternity that I lay on that board. But soon, I heard the familiar voice of the Pine Butte Ranch director. He came to me at once and knelt by my side.

"Leanne, I'm so sorry this happened to you and Anders. I heard about what you did to help everyone and I'm so grateful. Thank you." His presence was comforting and I reassured him that Anders and I were going to be just fine. He told me that the ranch was doing it's very best to reach Nathan and Carson, but so far, they hadn't made contact with them yet. The glacier lake they were hiking to was in a very remote location with no means of communication; cell phones were useless. A staff member planned to meet them at the trailhead and then drive them directly to the hospital; a forty mile distance.

I felt a little better with this news, however I knew it would be a difficult encounter for Nathan and Carson. I prayed for peace for my family as the news was shared with them.

Finally, it was time for Anders and me to be transported to the hospital. As the stretcher was lifted into the ambulance a wave of unexpected panic came over me and I said, "Wait! Wait, I don't think I can go right now. I'm not ready to ride in a car yet." The alarm and fear surprised me but after all, the last time I was in a vehicle, we were rolling and tumbling. So I guess it made some sense. The paramedics talked me through it and ever so gently slid me into the truck. But I felt no better; only worse. A sense of claustrophobia came over me and I felt like the ceiling was going to crush me. But I couldn't move to keep it from doing so. My arms were strapped down and the belts were incredibly tight, keeping me from taking a good, solid breath.

"I'm having trouble breathing. Help me please!" I begged. Anxiety took over and I began to sweat, tremble, and hyperventilate. I felt nauseous and started to cry. What was happening to me? And then, a voice of reason in my head spoke.

"Leanne, your son needs you. Be strong and courageous! You've got to keep it together for him. You can do this." I breathed in through my nose and out through my mouth at the coaching of the nearby paramedic and that helped for a few seconds. But for the majority of the ambulance ride, it was a battle between staying rational, and sinking into panic. I thought I might vomit so the paramedic loosened the straps a very small amount so I could gain a deeper breath, but not too much. Several times, I broke down crying as I shared bits and pieces from the accident. The paramedic held my hand, telling me it was all over now and that I had done the right thing. Every once in a while I called up to Anders who was sitting in the passenger seat to see how he was doing. In spite of how his mom was handling things, he was a trooper, even being allowed to operate the siren every few minutes.

After what seemed an eternity, we pulled into the Emergency Room Entrance at Teton Medical Center in Choteau, Montana. It felt so good to be lifted out of the crammed ambulance, to see the sky and take a breath of some fresh air; even if for only a few seconds. Our stats were rattled off by the paramedics to the hospital staff as Anders and I were both transported inside. I was relieved to know that they were still being cautious and giving Anders medical attention too. But quickly, the feeling of panic, and the inability to take a deep breath returned as I entered the building and bright lights, medical staff, new smells and sounds swirled around me. Tears streamed down my face.

I knew in my brain that the nightmare was over and we were finally in good hands. Yet, for some reason, my body decided that now was the time to go into panic mode and wrestle with fear. I didn't understand but tried my best to keep it under control. An ER nurse was comforting as she spoke.

"Just breathe, Leanne. Take a slow, deep breath; in through your nose and out through your mouth. Stay calm for us, all right?" I did as she advised and tried to focus on Anders.

"That's it. Inhale nice and slow. Good job, Leanne. Just breathe." My mind and my body were in conflict and I struggled in the fight. When would this nightmare come to an end?

Chapter 12

HEALING BEGINS

In the exam room, I was kept immobilized with a cervical collar until X-rays could be taken. Meanwhile, the doctor and nurses gave me a thorough assessment of other potential injuries. They told me I was going to be sore for a while with plenty of cuts, scrapes and bruises all over my body. When examining my feet, I heard lots of sympathetic sighs and concern from the nurses.

"What happened to your poor feet ma'am?" Apparently, they were swollen, blistered, bruised and full of cuts and rocks. I honestly had no idea! They brought over a lamp and spent some time cleaning them as best they could. My legs were also torn up pretty good and someone cleaned and bandaged them for me.

This was a small town hospital with only one X-ray machine and technician. The other victims were of higher priority, having arrived before me, so I had to wait a while for my turn. I couldn't get a good look at my surroundings. I could only listen and stare at the white ceiling. I learned that some of the other victims had been taken to a bigger facility in Great Falls, either by ambulance or helicopter. I worried about them. I worried about Nathan, Carson, and Ella and how they were receiving the news of the accident. I worried about Dan's family too and wondered how and when they would learn of his passing. So many things were swirling around in my head and I could only lay there. At times it was just too much to bear. Tears were flowing constantly. I am not normally an emotional person, but the trauma and the weight of what had happened that day was beginning to settle on my heart and mind. One kind nurse told me, "You need to have a good cry after all you've been through!"

As staff people came in and out of my room I would share details of the accident or ask if they knew anything about my family. And then finally, I received some good news. Anders had been cleared and officially discharged. He was allowed to sit in a chair next to me and that was a huge comfort. We held hands and he showed me his band aids.

"They gave me some medicine for my cuts but it didn't hurt." Then, he was given some coloring books, goldfish crackers, and apple juice from one of the nurses and seemed content to occupy himself with them. I wasn't able to turn my head and get a good look at him, but I imagined him sitting there with only a few little cuts and bruises. I thought about the miracle it was that God spared his life. Then images of Dan and the other injured passengers clouded my mind. Fresh tears formed as I relived the experience all over again.

There was a knock at the door from a nurse.

"Leanne? Your daughter is here now. Would you like me to send her in? I think she's pretty anxious to see you."

"Yes! Please!" I said enthusiastically. I couldn't wait to reassure and hold my girl. Soon I heard Ella tentatively ask for me.

"Mom?" Although I couldn't see her, I reached out my arms to her. She came running to my bedside and buried her face into my side. Anders joined us and it was a sweet reunion.

"Oh Daughter, I'm so sorry you had to worry about us. We're going to be alright." Ella was immediately concerned about the neck brace, but I told her that doctors were just being cautious.

"Mom, what happened to you guys? We waited so long for you to come!" I told her the basic story, not wanting to frighten her any more than she already had been. Later on I learned what her experience had been like and from the sound of it; she'd had a long, worrisome day too.

When the driver of the first van, Larry, noticed that he did not see the second van following in his rear view mirror he decided to wait at a stop sign assuming we'd catch up. It's common for vehicles to keep a distant length from one another on gravel roads. But when ten minutes went by and still our van never appeared, Larry thought that maybe we had stopped to see some wildlife. So he continued on to the cattle ranch. Once arriving at the destination, the group waited some more until it became very awkward for them. Eventually, Larry decided to leave his group at the ranch and see if our van had gotten a flat tire or something. A short time later, his heart sank as he came upon the scene of the crash. By that time, emergency personnel had arrived, making it clear the seriousness of the situation. Another woman from the tour group decided to follow Larry out of curiosity and came upon the crash scene as well. When she realized what had happened, she turned and drove back to the ranch tour group and hysterically told them all, including Ella, what she saw. This put everyone into a panic.

But Ella reassured me. "Mom, I was really glad that Giorgia's mom Carla was there to take care of me. She did everything you would have done. She hugged me, held my hand, prayed with me and sat with me the whole time."

I clung to my little girl and thanked God for the wonderful new friends we had made this week. He certainly was looking out for us in every single way.

Just then, a nurse came in and asked if I might be interested in having a hospital chaplain visit with us. I agreed and a few moments later a man came and pulled up a chair beside me. Ella shared a chair with Anders and they quietly colored together while I spoke with the pastor. He was kind and gentle and didn't probe with questions but let me speak only as I felt comfortable. I told him various details of the accident in between the tears, of my running for help and how I felt God's presence through it all. He asked if he could read some scripture to me and then brought out his Bible. I listened as he began.

Isaiah 43:1-2, *"Do not fear, for I have redeemed you; I have summoned you by name; you are mine. When you pass through the waters, I will be with you; and when you pass through the rivers, they will not sweep over you. ..."*

Overcome with emotion, I could barely speak. Those words were meant for me and it affirmed what I had felt all along; that God was indeed with me. He loved me and He protected me.

The chaplain then asked if he could pray for us. Ella perked up from where she was sitting and asked, "Can I pray with you too?" She and Anders joined in and we had a sweet moment of prayer in the hospital room. Not long after, it was time for me to go into X-ray. I was to have five images taken of my neck, jaw, arms and chest. It was in between images I was told that Nathan and Carson had finally arrived at the hospital. The technician gave us a few moments alone. My poor boys had absolutely no idea what they were walking into as they tentatively approached me. Later, they told me how it had unfolded for them.

As Nathan, Carson, and friends Joe and August were making their way back to the Pine Butte Guest Ranch after an exhilarating all day hike to Our Lake, a staff person met them along the driveway and solemnly gave them the news.

"There's been a rollover accident, with at least one fatality, involving one of the vans that went to the cattle ranch tour today. Nathan, your wife and son were involved. I don't know their condition other than it's pretty bad. I need you to come with me to the hospital right now." So Joe and August walked the rest of the way to the ranch while Nathan and Carson headed straight to the hospital, which was a forty-five minute drive. Nathan later told me what an agonizing trip that was. All kinds of thoughts raced through his mind as he worried about what he might find. Would Anders and I be alive? Unrecognizable? On life support? Then, he realized he needed to prepare Carson as well. It was a conversation he never expected or wanted to have with his son.

As they entered the imaging room, I was sitting in a wheelchair with the cervical collar still on. I could see their terrified faces as they tentatively approached so I gave them a reassuring smile and held out my hand.

"Anders checked out fine and they're just making sure I don't have any broken bones. Hopefully then, I can take this awful collar off soon." I said. Relief washed over both of them and they gave me a gentle hug.

Miraculously, my X-rays showed absolutely no fractures. Soon, I was signing discharge papers and being handed some pain medication and an antibiotic. The ER doctor considered keeping me overnight for observation but advised that with everything Anders and I had been through emotionally, being together as a family would probably be the best medicine of all. Before leaving though, I wanted to check on the other passengers and see for myself how they were coping. My last image of them was not a pretty picture and I needed to know they were okay.

I looked in on one of the women. She appeared so much better, out of her stained shirt and in a fresh, clean, hospital gown. Her face had been cleaned up and her arm was also carefully wrapped and clinging to her. I stroked her hair gently and told her I was so glad to see her. Next was the elderly man. He was just getting off the phone with his son. It was so good to see him nestled against some clean pillows with his legs stretched out properly, on the dry blankets. I kissed his cheek and said, "You look a lot more comfortable than you did in that van. Now, get some rest, and no more tumbling for a while." The other passengers had been sent to another, larger hospital in Great Falls so I would have to ask about their status later.

As our family exited the ER, I was surprised and touched to find that the waiting room was filled with all of the other passengers who had ridden in the first van. They were very concerned but thankful to see Anders and me as the first patients discharged. There was even a little cheer as we came into the room. We stood around for a few minutes giving hugs and words of comfort and then a nurse interrupted, handing me a bag with our belongings in it. I peeked inside and noticed my one black sandal that I had pulled from the creek was missing.

"Shoot, my sandal isn't in here. I wonder what happened to it. I thought I had it in the ambulance with me."

"Oh that?" Nathan piped in. "Well, I noticed you only had one and it was all muddy so I threw it away. I figured there wasn't any point in keeping one shoe anyway."

Disappointment filled me. It may sound silly but for whatever reason, that sandal was a trophy to me; evidence that I had survived the crash and ran barefoot. It was a symbol of my testimony that God was with me every step of the way. I asked Nathan which trash can he put it in and he stopped in his tracks giving me the, "Are you serious?" look. Deep down, I knew he was right. A hospital garbage container was a cesspool for germs and bacteria; definitely not a place to go dumpster diving. So I relented, sucking up tears of frustration. It was time to leave.

Pulling into the familiar driveway of the guest ranch felt good. As I stepped out of our van, I took a deep breath of that wonderful, sweet smelling air and it gave me peace. Other guests and staff members were anxiously waiting for our return and they came to meet us with hugs and warm wishes. By this time dinner was long past but none of us had much of an appetite. Heading straight to our cabin sounded most inviting. The ranch gardener, Sheryl, thoughtfully delivered fresh baked cookies and lemonade to our door. As she stood there, she comforted me by sharing her belief that Dan knew God. This news meant so much to me. Witnessing a man lose his life was absolutely traumatic. But realizing that he had been welcomed into the arms of his Heavenly Father made the truth easier to accept. I hugged her and thanked her for telling me those things. Nathan excused himself to the ranch office, so he could telephone our family members back in Wisconsin and fill them in on what had happened. And then we all tried desperately to get some rest that night.

Anders slept between me and Nathan, but it's hard to say if any of us ever really got any decent amount of sleep. Every time I closed my eyes I had visions of Dan in the water. Sometimes reality was replaced with false images and I would see Anders buckled and submerged underwater instead. The fear was absolutely overwhelming and I felt like I was drowning myself. Tears, trembling, and nightmares plagued me. I could tell Anders was experiencing much of the same as he moaned and sometimes cried out in fear. I would reach out to him by putting my hand on his back and whisper words of comfort.

The one thing Anders said to me before drifting off to sleep was almost a scold and it took me by surprise because he hadn't really said much about the events of the day.

"Mom, I told you I wanted to ride in the other van. But you wouldn't let me!"

I didn't allow myself to get defensive. He was just a child processing an extremely difficult experience and I was thankful he voiced these thoughts so we could talk about it.

"Anders, I know that what we went through was really scary and terrible. And I'm so sorry. But I think that God needed us to be in that van for a reason. You and I were the only ones who didn't get hurt, right? And that meant we could help everybody else." Anders' attitude changed as he seemed to accept my answer.

"Okay, Mommy." He said as he burrowed down next to me.

In the morning, it was a relief to see the sun, knowing the long hours of darkness were over. Nathan was already out of bed but Anders was thankfully sound asleep. I was grateful to see his little chest rising and falling after such a fitful night. I stared at him, almost taken aback that he was alive and next to me. I started to sit up and then realized I would need to take it slow as my body ached considerably. I knew I needed to take another dose of pain medication. As my feet touched the hardwood floor, I absent-mindedly put weight on them. Quickly, I retracted them in pain, recalling the state they were in. Just then Nathan entered the room and brought me several pairs of soft hospital socks to slip on. We had twenty-four hours left of our stay at Pine Butte Guest Ranch. I spent most of my time sitting on the front porch of the main lodge, soaking in the sights of the mountains, breathing in the fresh air and resting. It was hard to believe that just a few days earlier, I was sitting in that same spot with Dan. The mood at the ranch was somber although there were still wonderful memories to be made. Our kids, including Anders, and their friends Giorgia and August, swam in the pool, played with the horses, and fished in the streams that final day. We all enjoyed deliciously cooked meals in the dining hall with our friends in spite of the missing people that still remained hospitalized. During one of our final meals, the ranch director shared a few meaningful words with our group regarding the events that had taken place and then he read a heartfelt email sent that morning from Dan's wife, Susan. My prayers went out to her and the rest of Dan's family as they dealt with the shocking loss.

A ranch staff person had spent some time that afternoon at the accident site and then later the junk yard where the van had been towed, looking for lost articles from the passengers. He came back to the ranch and opened up his trunk showing us what he had come up with. In it was an iPad, some boots, a backpack and a few other miscellaneous things. I hobbled over to see what else I could find and was thrilled to see my other black sandal!

"Oh, my shoe! Where did you find this?" I asked. Apparently, it had been recovered from the bottom of the van. I held on to it like a well-earned medal. I would be able to have my tangible proof after all. To this day, I can't fully explain why it means so much to have that sandal, but when I see it, I remember what Anders and I went through, and automatically, I thank God. To me it's an important reminder of survival and His mercy.

That final evening, a Teton County Sheriff came out to the ranch and asked to interview me. He recorded our conversation and I was a little nervous. But at the same time everything was very fresh in my mind and I knew I could convey a clear and accurate picture for him. There was only one question I struggled to answer.

"Were you and your son wearing seat belts at the time of the accident?" My heart sank because the answer was no.

"We were not." I said. I didn't hesitate to give him a truthful reply but my shame was evident. Call it vacation mode, or being naive to think that nothing could happen to us in the middle of nowhere. Whatever my reasoning, I experienced tremendous guilt. *What kind of mother was I not to seat belt my own child?* I thought as I shook my head.

But honestly, *wearing* a seat belt was part of the nightmare that plagued me. I constantly thought, "What if Anders and I *were* wearing our seat belts? Seeing Dan strapped in his safety belt, hanging upside down, with his head underwater was a disturbing sight; one I fought to get out of my mind persistently. Could that have been Anders and I if we had been wearing our seat belts too? I thought about if I had been belted and suspended with *my* head underwater; would I have had the presence of mind to realize what had just occurred, know where I was, and how to get out? Or would I have gulped in water and panicked? These were things I wrestled with for many months afterwards. Still, did I believe in the importance and necessity of seat belts? Absolutely I did! And from then on, there would never *ever* be a day that I would ignore them. Did I think that maybe this was the .0001% chance when *not* wearing a seat belt went in our favor? It's possible. However, wearing a belt could have prevented us all from being thrown about inside the van. What I do believe, with my whole being, is that God miraculously spared our group from being ejected from the vehicle, leaving Anders and I basically unscathed. This allowed me to assist others and go for help. If Anders had been seriously injured or worse, I don't know that I would have paid much attention to anyone else, or left him there alone. And obviously, if I was injured, I couldn't have made the run. Many "what ifs" tortured me, both day and night. I replayed the events over and over again and thought about what I could have done differently. But after I completed my testimony with the sheriff, he said to me, "Ma'am, you did everything you could to help. It's pretty remarkable and I'm confident you did the right thing."

I certainly wasn't looking to be made a hero, but this gave me comfort because I questioned some of my actions such as, "Did I really try my absolute hardest to free Dan?" And, "Maybe I shouldn't have moved Arthur like I did. What if he had a broken neck?" Or, "Why didn't I wrap up that woman's wrist with my shirt to help curb the bleeding?" But the sheriff's words put those thoughts aside for the time being and gave me some reassurance. I had done all I could.

Finally, Sunday morning arrived and it was time to head home. Tearful goodbyes were exchanged and it was difficult leaving the ranch even though the thought of home sounded sweet. We had bonded with this group of vacationers and staff, experiencing extreme highs and lows that would remain in our hearts for a lifetime.

Little did our family realize when I prayed an unassuming prayer our very first night at the ranch that God was going to answer it in such an extraordinary way...

> *"Lord, I'm in awe that we get to be here in this beautiful place. Thank you. And I sense that you brought us here for a reason. I think it's more than just simply to enjoy a family vacation and your beautiful creation. While we're here, I pray that our family could be a witness for you, and an encouragement to the staff and other guests. Please use us. Amen"*

We would never forget these amazing people or this incredible place.

~

For me, the drive back home was an emotional one. I startled easily; especially in the van. I didn't like sharp turns, a faster speed than was necessary, or when Nathan needed to brake suddenly. I struggled being a passenger, even though Nathan was one of the most cautious and safest drivers I'd ever known. At times, I felt better if I was behind the wheel because then I could be in control. Once we reached an area where there was cell service, we were able to start making phone calls to family, giving them more details and letting them know our travel status. Everyone wanted to know what had happened, including the media. Several Montana newspapers got my name and contact information and wanted to report more on the story of, "*Woman, Barefoot, Runs for Help After Crash*".

I didn't mind speaking to them. To me, it was even therapeutic and I held nothing back in sharing how my faith in God carried me through that horrific ordeal. "He was with me on that gravel road, every step of the way." I told the reporters. Social media and some of our local Wisconsin papers also shared the story and our community and friends back home were hearing of the experience as well.

It seemed helpful to talk about the accident; to process it and share the extraordinary and miraculous experience with others. But at the same time I was still a fragile, leaky faucet, with tears flowing often and sometimes unexpectedly. Flashbacks from the crash plagued me and I found it difficult to escape them.

One week after the accident, my family attended a birthday party for our little neighbor girl, Willow Stenberg. When I learned that it was to be held at Interstate Beach, I cringed, knowing that the water clarity there can be brownish in color, closely resembling the creek our van plunged in. I worried that this might trigger some difficult memories from the accident. But I knew my kids wanted to go and the Stenbergs were such special friends to us. Hesitantly, I attended the beach party with my kids in spite of my anxiety-filled spirit. In the beginning, things went okay and I stayed near the picnic tables, chatting with other moms and helping with the food. But when the kids went off to swim in the lake, the adults sat along the shore keeping a watchful eye on them, and that's when my anxiety level began to rise. Among splashing and swimming, one of the children innocently did a dead-mans' float. She was just playing around, but this set me off into an outright panic attack and I ran into a public restroom, hyperventilating, crying uncontrollably and trembling. I know it was irrational but the images caused such fear.

Another time I had a near panic attack when I was driving my children down the interstate. I happened to be following a vehicle just like the van we crashed in. I kept picturing it veering off the road with my children inside of it. It was terrifying! Thankfully I was able to talk myself down from it and gain some control while still behind the wheel.

I dreaded nighttime the most because darkness seemed to fuel my wandering imagination. I decided to contact a therapist from our local clinic and she confirmed that after what Anders and I had been through, the Post Traumatic Stress Symptoms I was experiencing were completely normal. I could expect them for a few weeks. She encouraged me that they should begin to diminish after about a month, but warned that if they do *not* subside, counseling was recommended. This advice was very comforting and reassuring to me. I wasn't losing my mind!

Anders on the other hand was managing things very differently from me. He did not appreciate everyone's interest in the accident or see the need to discuss it. Whenever he heard me speak of it he would leave the room. And if this wasn't possible, he would put a jacket or blanket over his head or even put his hand over my mouth to make me stop talking. His way of coping was to ignore or just pretend it never happened. This concerned Nathan and me. We tried to help him work through it somehow, but we also wondered if forcing him to discuss it might be harmful. So instead we waited, observed and prayed for him. People kept reminding us how resilient kids were. "He'll be fine. Just give him some time." We hoped that was true for Anders.

Another person who I was concerned about after the accident was actually someone I had never even met. It was the wife of the van driver, Susan Imming. A man had tragically died a few days ago leaving behind a beloved wife, children, and grandchildren. Yes, the victims in his passenger van had all been hurt and injured. But his family just lost someone incredibly special to them. They never even got to say goodbye! What a heartbreaking way to lose someone. I wanted to somehow reach out to this woman and her family and offer some kind of comfort- to tell her my belief that Dan had not suffered. In my humble opinion, he was already gone when I reached his side and tried to save him. I also wanted to let her know that Anders and I were alright and we realized this was just a terrible accident. We understood that Dan didn't mean for any of this to happen. Most of all, we were very sorry for her loss.

I was able to get contact information from the ranch and I sent Susan an email a few days after our return home. About a day later I was surprised to see that she had replied. In corresponding, we gave each other a gift. I felt a connection with Dan and his family, and in return, she was able to learn some special things about her husband's final days on earth. I told her about our evening spent on the front porch, watching the sunset as hummingbirds buzzed by, and how he and Larry co-led our family on a spectacular glacier-lake hike.

Susan and I kept up communication via email and became friends on Facebook. It was good therapy for us both. I learned that Dan had been a firefighter with the Elk Creek Fire Department for more than thirty years with the district, filling roles as Lieutenant, Captain and Deputy Chief. He was the father of two sons and a daughter, and grandfather to five grandchildren. I also discovered online that several Colorado newspapers featured stories about his life and legacy. I was inspired by what was written by Editor Walter L. Newton of *The Flume,* Park County Colorado. It made me wish I had known Dan longer.

> *"Some heroes are almost invisible while giving their time, sweat and love to the community. Daniel Imming, 73, was one of those heroes. … Dan was always there when you needed him, always uplifting*

> *you when talking with him; he was always the first to*
> *help. … He was deeply respected by all who knew him.*

Dan's wife, Susan invited me to his memorial service in Conifer, Colorado. As I sought some kind of closure to the accident ordeal, I considered the cost of airfare and lodging but realized it was just too much. However, a few weeks after his funeral, she thoughtfully sent me a program and lovely photograph of Dan. I'm so glad she did because *that* picture was how I wanted to remember him.

Chapter 18

ORCHESTRATED BY GOD

hankfully, our family had two positive distractions to help with the effects of the accident. The first was a neighborhood carnival I had planned. I thought it would be something fun to do with my kids. When we first moved into our cul-de-sac neighborhood in 2009, I had always imagined it being the ideal place to hold such an event. My vision was to have games and concessions set up all around the paved cul-de-sac with tables where families could sit at in the center. The little trails between our house and Stenbergs would be perfect for pony rides; that is, if I could find a pony. As plans were made to have the carnival that fall, my hope was that it could generate some funds to donate to the Cystic Fibrosis Foundation. Eventually, my event became known as the Carnival for CF.

My personal expectation was to draw about 100 to 150 people and make somewhere around $1,000. But as my idea spread, the in-kind donations began to pour in: food, paper products, carnival prizes, volunteers, services and some really, *really* nice silent auctions prizes. So I began to think beyond just a simple kiddy carnival and see what God could do. Local businesses, the schools, churches, scouts, and athletic teams all offered to pitch in. People were getting really enthusiastic about this! I was too, although the practical side of me was also concerned about the weather and things beyond my control. What if I went through all of this work only to have it rained out? I used to be a wedding coordinator and I always tried to talk brides out of having outdoor ceremonies and receptions for this very reason.

But the Lord was gracious as He orchestrated an absolutely perfect day for us. On September 14, 2014, with the help of my husband, friends and dozens of volunteers, we hosted quite an event in our small town. I was the ringmaster of sorts as I oversaw more than twenty-five games and activities throughout our neighborhood cul-de-sac including face painting, temporary tattoos, balloon sculptures with Ben the balloon man, spin art, cakewalk, fish pond, pony rides, inflatables, spin the wheel, human hamster balls, archery, silent auction, basketball, a pie-in-the-face contest, live music, and an amphibian demonstration from Randy the Frog Guy, a local celebrity of sorts. There was popcorn, hotdogs, brats, chips, cotton candy, fountain pop, and mini donuts for sale. We even rented two porta-potties, to accommodate the large expected turn-out. Thanks to volunteers from the St. Croix Falls High school track team, the High School Football Cheerleading squad, our church youth group, and even a willing student who dressed up as The Amazing Spiderman, we pulled it off. When all was said and done, we had an overwhelming 500+ in attendance, bringing in more than $11,000 with 100% of the proceeds going to the Cystic Fibrosis Foundation! It was mind-blowing. A highlight for me was having an adorable, gray colored pony in my front yard along with a cotton-candy machine; two of my favorite things. I thought I might actually burst with happiness as my childhood dream played out before my eyes! So what if I was thirty-seven years old. The only depressing detail was that I was too heavy to actually sit on the pony. I settled for a picture, taken alongside her as I proudly held my towering stick of fluffy, pink, cotton-candy. All three of our kids had a blast helping to facilitate games, stuffing their faces with junk food, and getting in on the action. It was a great night and our tiny community really showed up in a big way. It felt like a gigantic hug. After the success of the carnival, people kept asking me, "You're doing this again next year, right?" But I decided that to avoid the need for marriage counseling, I should probably end on a positive note and never have a carnival in my front yard again.

Another positive distraction happened just two weeks after the carnival and was a complete surprise to our kids. Nathan and I had known for some time that Make-A-Wish planned to grant Anders' wish in the very near future. No, they weren't going to turn our basement into a gigantic saltwater aquarium for Flipper to live in. But they did plan to whisk our entire family of five away to Hawaii for a whole week! Mike and Holly had given us the dates and flight information. But other than that, we were really clueless as to our accommodations, and itinerary. In a lot of ways, the trip was a surprise to Nathan and me as well!

A few times a month, our family, along with our neighbors, liked to indulge at a local pizza place, taking advantage of their weekly special. So on the evening of October 3, 2014, it wasn't unusual for us to tell the kids that we were headed to Schooney's Pizza in downtown Taylors Falls, Minnesota, for supper. What they didn't know was that I had gone there earlier that day and decorated the restaurant with Hawaiian tablecloths, garland, coconuts and other novelty items. I also happened to invite about thirty of our closest friends and family to celebrate Anders' Make-A-Wish granting party. That night, as the kids strolled into our usual pizza place hangout, they were all completely taken aback as dozens of familiar, happy faces greeted them, including our wish-grantors, Mike and Holly Jones.

"Surprise! Guess what kind of party *this* is Anders!" Holly asked him. Our son was hesitant for about half a second and then his face lit up as he realized what was taking place. Carson had his wish party already, and now it was finally *his* turn! This was the moment he had been waiting for.

It was a memorable and exciting night as Anders learned that in less than thirty-six hours, our whole family would be boarding a plane for the island of Oahu! We would be swimming with dolphins, taking an excursion on a pirate ship, snorkeling, body surfing, and attending an authentic luau. It was all so exciting!

A day and a half later, a sleek, black limousine pulled up in our driveway at 9:00 AM sharp. It's not often a car like *that* is seen in our neck of the woods. I think you could have heard our eager squealing from a mile away. Never in our wildest dreams did we imagine such indulgence. And for the next seven days, our family embarked on a journey that is hard to put into words. My thesaurus is failing me as I search for adjectives to describe properly just how thrilled and awestruck we all were. At the same time we felt honored, humbled, and beyond grateful to experience such an opportunity. What a gift! Make-A-Wish thought of everything, making the trip personal and memorable for Anders specifically. I believe that God had a hand in this trip for several reasons.

When it was time to hash out dates for the trip, Make-A-Wish asked that we avoid the holiday seasons. *Our* only request was to find a week when our kids might have a day or two off of school in the hope that they wouldn't get too far behind in their studies. Make-A-Wish came back with a particular week in October and it worked great with our schedule.

As we looked forward to the experience, we knew it would be good therapy, not only for Anders, but for our entire family. We all had suffered tremendously as both boys were diagnosed with CF and our lives were turned upside down adjusting to a new normal. But we had no idea how much we would need this vacation after the terrible van accident that took place just eight weeks prior to leaving for Hawaii. I'll admit, I had some reservations about going on another family trip so soon after our ranch experience. I tried not to be irrational, but couldn't help but think, "What are the odds that something will go terribly wrong?" I know Nathan was wondering too, but we kept those thoughts to ourselves and pushed away the worry. Ultimately, peaceful rest and tranquility would be a very welcome sight.

Our first morning in Hawaii was an early one. We were still on Wisconsin time and the five hour difference was quite an adjustment for us. Plus, we were just a wee bit anxious to hit the beach and experience our first full day in paradise. We had the lagoon to ourselves and the kids tested the water. To their delight, it was warm and they regretfully wished, in a rather noisy way, that they had put their swimming suits on *before* coming down. We reminded them with parental shushing that it wasn't even 6:00 AM Hawaii time, and to try and be respectful of guests that were still sleeping. They waded on tiptoes, with their shorts pulled as high as they could go, while marveling and pointing at colorful fish all in the cove. It was like *Finding Nemo* out there as they spotted clown fish, blue tang, yellow tang, puffer fish, butterfly fish, angelfish, and more. It was incredible! I sat on the beach enjoying my kids' reactions equally as much as the view of the lagoon. Suddenly, there was a notification from Facebook Messenger on my phone. I have to admit I'm one of those who are tied to their phone. And it's possible that I might be slightly addicted to social media. The impulse to look at my phone was strong, even in the midst of all the tropical wonder. I told myself, "Leanne, you're in Hawaii on a Make-A-Wish trip of a life time with your family. Ignore the phone for a few days and pay attention to what is truly important!" But my curiosity got the best of me and I glanced down, rationalizing, "I'll just see who it's from." That's when I about fell off my beach chair. Expecting to see a message from a close friend or family member, wishing us well on our vacation, I was floored to see a lengthy message from Susan Imming, the wife of the van driver who died in Montana. I *had* to read it right then.

"Aloha Leanne,

So happy you are in Honolulu with Make-A-Wish! You guys deserve it and more. How long will you be there? Where are you staying? You won't believe this but I am flying to Honolulu tomorrow on a trip Dan

and I planned before his accident. I would love to at
least say hello if feasible, knowing your schedule is
likely very full. Also I don't have a car so it may be a
challenge. I am staying in Honolulu until Oct 11, then
going to Maui. This is surreal. I think of you and your
family every day, especially when I think of Dan. You
are amazing. … Let me know your plans and dates.
It would be so wonderful to meet you all in person if
it can work out! Mahalo,

Susan"

My eyes were wide as I realized what she was saying. Susan was planning to be in Hawaii, on the same island, during the exact same time period as us! How incredible was that? I gasped in amazement, which drew Nathan's attention.

"What's the matter?" He asked, with concern in his voice. I ran over to him and shared the unbelievable news. The circumstances were absolutely astounding. He was as blown away as I and we both agreed that we would make everything possible to see her. I wrote Susan back immediately.

"Susan that is incredible! We want to meet you too and
will do all we can to make that happen. We are staying
on Oahu. What time do you arrive? We have a rental
vehicle so we will be happy to come to you."

After some further correspondence, we made plans to meet for lunch at her hotel on Waikiki beach just two days later. I was eager but also nervous about the meeting. I knew this was going to be emotional. But would it be *too* emotional and difficult for her to see us? After all, Anders and I were the last ones to be with her husband, Dan, before he died. Would she ask us questions about the accident?

Or want to know if I had really done all I could to save him? The last thing I wanted to do was cause her more pain or suffering.

There was no denying that this meeting was an absolute miracle; her traveling all the way from Colorado and us from Wisconsin, coming together unknowingly on the island of Oahu, Hawaii! I knew this wasn't some chance encounter, but instead, completely orchestrated by God. And for some reason He wanted us to meet one another in person. I told Susan this and she seemed to agree. Her enthusiasm to see us was reciprocated through our messaged communication.

Over the two days, as our family relished the time in Hawaii, the upcoming encounter with Susan was a constant presence in my mind. Knowing that God wanted us to meet her and had specifically chosen this time, and this place, was incredible to me.

Finally, the day arrived and we were able to find her hotel which was impressively located in an upscale part of downtown Honolulu, among fantastic designer shopping and lavish places to eat. Expensive cars, interesting people, and unique sights were everywhere. It was a spectacular scene and we were all a little star struck as we got out of our vehicle. Susan had told me in a text message that she'd be out in front of her hotel waiting for us and although I wasn't really sure what she looked like, I knew the moment I saw a slight, brunette-haired woman standing along the sidewalk that it was her. As our family approached her, I waved and she smiled large and bright. Any apprehension I had felt before our meeting quickly melted away as I hurried my pace and we embraced. It was as if we were dear friends; family even, hugging with tears in our eyes. I introduced Susan to Nathan and our children. When I got to Anders, she bent down to his level and shook his hand.

"Hi Anders. I've heard so much about you. It's really nice to meet you!" He smiled and returned a polite response. "How do you like Hawaii so far?" Susan asked. Anders had no problem telling her all about his favorite experiences on the island. Susan was excited to listen as she ushered us into her beautiful hotel filled with marble columns, vibrant flower gardens, and fabulous water features. Eventually, we gathered around a luncheon table that faced the sparkling, turquoise colored sea. The wonder of it all was almost overwhelming and we marveled at the incredible surroundings!

Conversation was light and easy as we took turns sharing and getting to know each other. A server came to the table and we placed our order and then decided to let the kids wander a short distance from the table to watch some of the surfing action happening on Waikiki beach while our food was being prepared. My hope was that with the kids temporarily away, Susan would feel more comfortable if she had some personal things on her heart that she wanted to say or ask. As expected, our conversation turned to Dan.

"It's been exactly two months since he's been gone and I'm finally, just now, feeling like I can grieve his absence. Things were so hectic at first with the shock of his death, and friends and family all wanting to come and spend time with me. And then of course, we had his funeral a month later. Now, life is beginning to calm down and I'm realizing, he's actually gone, and I'm alone." She choked up at this and I saw the anguish in her face. I couldn't imagine losing my husband so suddenly like that. What a brave thing she had done coming all this way to Hawaii by herself. She and Dan had planned this trip together many months before his unexpected passing.

I took her hand and said, "I'm so glad you came on this trip Susan. I really believe this is going to be an important time for you to grieve, heal, and feel close to Dan. He would have wanted you to come." She nodded in agreement. Susan went on to share what it had been like to receive the news of his passing.

"I was standing in the checkout at a Staples office supply store when I got the phone call." Her pain was still fresh. And then she went on to say, "I'm just so sorry that you and Anders had to be a part of the accident."

I stopped her right there. "Susan, I want you to know that I am at peace with it; all of it. I believe God put me there for a reason and he protected me and Anders. We're okay! God gave me the strength to do what I had to do and get help for the others. And God gave Anders the strength to stay calm and be brave." She nodded while pondering my words. We talked some more about Dan and what he was like. She helped us learn new things about him like how they got involved at the Pine Butte Guest Ranch and their shared love for the outdoors.

When the server brought us our food, the kids came back to the table and excitedly told us about the surfing and waves. The surf here was much stronger than our resort's secluded lagoon and the whitecaps it produced were impressive. Once they realized that food was in front of them, they began eating and we were able to continue our conversation.

"Tell me about Dan's funeral." I asked Susan. Reminiscing, she gave a sigh and smiled.

"In some ways it felt more like a celebration than a funeral. The gathering of friends, family, and fellow firefighters who came was simply overwhelming. I think we estimated 600 in attendance. The service was crowded but it was really lovely. We had it in a church. I'm not very religious myself and it wouldn't have mattered to me *where* we had the funeral but I know that Dan would have wanted it that way so we held it at Our Lady of the Pines Catholic Church." At her mention of this, I wondered if this was the reason God allowed us to cross paths with Susan. I was struck by how God deeply loves His children and actively pursues them. I let her continue.

"The tribute paid to him as a volunteer firefighter was so touching. Dan was given full honors, having served for over thirty years. Firefighters from several departments came dressed in uniform. There were bagpipes and an Honor Guard. One of the most moving times in the service was toward the end. Tradition is that when a fallen firefighter is laid to rest, the fire dispatch will issue final tones and a ceremonial last call. At that moment, there wasn't a dry eye in the building."

"I'm sure that was very honoring to him." Nathan said and I

nodded in agreement, trying to picture what that solemn moment must have been like.

The rest of our lunch and conversation with Susan was really special. It never felt awkward or uncomfortable even though we had only just met. Maybe it was because we all knew this encounter had been divinely arranged, causing us to find true meaning in our visit. As the meal was winding down, Nathan took the kids to the restroom and left Susan and I alone at the table. She took the opportunity to say to me,

"Leanne, I just don't know how you do it; how you've dealt with it all. Having two children with a terrible disease, and then the accident. ... It's just so much to handle."

She was right. I could have been dealing with everything that happened that spring and summer much differently. I tried to explain how I felt.

"The truth is, without God, I would be a mess! He has been my rock as we've gone through our various trials. Many people think we should have an easy and wonderful life here on earth. But nowhere in the Bible does it say that. It actually says we will have many troubles. But thankfully, what God *does* promise us is that He will be *with* us through those troubles. He also promises us the hope of heaven, if we trust in His Son Jesus. And that is how I've been able to put one foot in front of the other, literally, as I ran down that gravel road for help. It's also what gets me up in the morning and not fear my sons' illnesses or their shortened life expectancies; knowing there is more than just the here and now. That is what gives me peace." Susan didn't question my reasoning, but simply contemplated what I had to say. I took comfort, knowing I had shared my heart without reservation.

Nathan and the kids came back and with our lunch finished we moved to a pretty place with a view of the ocean and took pictures together so we could forever remember our remarkable meeting with our new friend. We strolled along the busy beach and then headed back along the downtown strip toward the area where our vehicle was parked. Just before parting ways, Susan took something out of her pocket.

"Anders, as you know, my husband Dan was a firefighter for many years. And firemen must be incredibly brave to do their job. You too were very brave on the day of the accident. So I want you to have this." Susan then pulled out an envelope and inside was a patch and a card. She read it aloud to us all as we stood on the street corner, oblivious to the traffic and noise.

> *"Dear Anders, You are my hero! Thank you so much for helping everyone during the accident at Pine Butte. I am so sorry it happened and I hope you are getting better. This patch is for you. It is from the Elk Creek Fire Rescue Department where Dan volunteered for more than thirty years. You are so brave!*
>
> *Hugs and Love,*
> *Susan.*

She then presented the colorful, embroidered patch to Anders, pointing out its words and importance. It was just like the one from Dan's own firefighter uniform. It read:

ELK CREEK FIRE RESCUE, CONIFER, COLORADO, ESTABLISHED IN 1948.

Nathan and I were too choked up to speak. It was a beautiful gesture; one that our seven-year-old boy wouldn't fully grasp, but we certainly did. Susan was overcome with emotion and we took turns hugging her. It was difficult to say goodbye but I knew that we would stay in touch. God had orchestrated this special connection with her and I wanted to make sure we kept it.

Susan, Anders and Leanne near Waikiki Beach.

The remainder of our trip to Hawaii was incredible. We soaked up as much of the warm ocean, white, sandy beaches, and lush green foliage as we could in those seven days. A highlight for the entire family was the dolphin experience at Sea Life Aquarium where Anders, our animal lover, finally got to meet face to face with a 450 pound gentle giant named Maui. All five of us were able to wade into the salt water pool to interact with the beautiful creature. My face was a mixture of salty water and salty tears as I witnessed my son's dream come true. I think Anders would agree that experiencing dolphins in Hawaii was far better than having one live in our basement. I knew we all would treasure the memory of that week forever.

Chapter 14

THE COURAGE TO FACE HIS FEAR

U pon returning home from Hawaii, we attempted to slide into the most normal routine that CF could allow. After all of the incredible highs and lows we'd been through over the past year, it would actually be good to have some mundane days for a change. But as school and fall activities revved up for the year, it became clear that something wasn't quite right emotionally with our youngest son.

At first it was small incidences that we tried to pass off as nothing. Like the time he stayed overnight at his best friend Ethan's house. Oddly, I received a phone call around 9:00 PM that evening saying Anders wanted us to come get him. His reasons waffled between a tummy ache and missing us and didn't seem legitimate. This kind of behavior was unusual for him. He had always been our self-assured kid and he loved being with friends, especially Ethan. Anders had spent many nights at his house in the past and I felt completely confident knowing he was in a safe place. I tried my best to console him over the phone. However, in the end we relented, driving out into the night to bring Anders home. Our hope was that this was simply a one-time case of homesickness.

But in other areas of his life, we witnessed our normally confident, happy-go-lucky child, become increasingly anxious and withdrawn. He lost interest in playing with friends and he was having trouble sleeping at night. Anders normally looked forward to Saturday mornings in the fall because it meant taking part in his favorite sport, football. In fact, our seven-year-old had big aspirations to become a professional football player for the Minnesota Vikings someday. Usually, going to play community flag football with about sixty-five other elementary kids was pretty important to him. But one Saturday morning as we walked him across the field toward his team, he started to mutter things like,

"I don't want to play football today. I want to stay home with you instead." We brushed it off and kept walking. He became more insistent and paranoid about not wanting to be at practice and then suddenly he just dropped to the ground, curled in a fetal position, trembling, crying, and begging us not to leave him alone. He seemed absolutely terrified! Nathan and I were perplexed at this bizarre behavior in the middle of the grassy field, with children and parents all around us. It was not like Anders, our typical tough-guy to do such a thing. I crouched down so he could hear me.

"Bubba, we're not going to leave you. We'll stay on the sidelines like we always do and watch you play. You love football! Why are you so scared?" At this point Anders was hysterical and sobbing. I scooped him up and took him back to the van so he could calm down and not cause a scene. Once in the safety and comfort of our vehicle I asked him to take some deep breaths. I found some tissues and helped him blow his nose. He responded to this and stopped crying. But he was unable to articulate why he was so frightened of being left alone. It was very strange. There had been no indication of this unexpected episode before heading to the football field. It was like a switch turned on and suddenly he was terrified of something. But we didn't know what it was exactly. Eventually, we were able to talk Anders into doing what he loved and participate in football practice. But he held our hands and hugged us several times before joining his teammates in warm-ups. We assured him we'd be close by watching along the side lines. My heart ached as I observed him and wondered what was going on inside his little mind.

Bed time was becoming more and more difficult as well. When the lights would go out, Anders was no longer comfortable in his own bed. He had trouble falling asleep and when he did, it was fitful and he would sometimes wake from a seemingly bad dream. More and more, we found him coming up to our bedroom and asking to sleep with us. The first few times I willingly turned down the covers and warmly welcomed our "baby" into bed, much to Nathan's chagrin. I'll admit that a part of me enjoyed having him snuggle in with us. Anders knew how to pull at my mama heart-strings. He'd burrow into me and wrap his arms around my neck whispering that I was the best mom ever. I'd melt and think, "How sweet, my baby needs me." Knowing how fast kids grow up, I'd wonder, "How many more times will Anders want to snuggle with me?" Of course Nathan didn't find this as sweet. Because when I'd have Anders' head near mine, Nathan would end up with Anders' butt and feet. Often times getting kicked in places men don't appreciate. So the enjoyment was sucked out for us all. We tried hard to get Anders to sleep in his own bed. It felt like we were dealing with a toddler once again. Being firm, praying with him, offering a drink, plugging in night lights, playing music, or stories on CD didn't seem to make a difference. Anders was becoming irrational with his fears at night. It was more than just him manipulating us into letting him sleep in a warm cozy bed with his mama. He was literally terrified of being alone. We would find him trembling, panicking, and hyperventilating even.

The last straw was when Anders began to experience separation anxiety in common places like church and school. When it came time to drop him off for various activities, he'd become almost nonsensical, displaying panic and fear. Our daily routines were being interrupted constantly. We were at a loss at what to do and began to worry for Anders.

Then it dawned on me. Could it be our son was dealing with something far more serious and real than just homesickness or a phase? Was it possible he was holding onto fear from the van accident we survived in Montana? I thought about the traumatic separation he experienced when I left him at the scene and ran for help. As the realization came over me, I pictured him standing alone on that gravel road, with a bloody and bewildered face. He didn't want me to leave him. But he stood bravely anyway, knowing he had a job to do: watch for cars and wave them down. Meanwhile an overturned van sat in a muddy creek below him, while a deceased man's body lay visible and five other passengers struggled in pain and injury. I later learned that no one ever comforted Anders while I was gone. How could they? Each of them was so involved in their own suffering. Did I blame them? No. But I felt a deep sadness and even guilt for the anguish that Anders had endured and was continuing to bear from that point on. It was time to finally get him the professional help he deserved.

I contacted Melissa, who referred us to a Psychologist, Dr. April Wallace from St. Croix Regional Medical Center. We were told that April was difficult to get into so I prepared myself for a long wait. But by God's grace, she had a cancellation for the very next day and Anders was able to see her. I had a talk with him the night before the appointment, explaining what kind of doctor April was and why Daddy and I thought it was a good idea to visit her. I told Anders about the possibility that she may ask some questions about the van accident. His eyes got big.

"Why would she want to talk about *that*? I don't think I'll go. Do I have to?" he asked.

I sighed. My poor son had been through so much. His usual response when the subject of the accident came up was to leave the room, place his hand over my mouth, or, if none of these options were possible, put an article of clothing or a blanket over his head. So why would he want to discuss it with a complete stranger? But I had confidence that April would know best how to deal with Anders and be able to draw out his feelings somehow. I hugged my son tightly and told him I would be with him and that if he didn't want to talk about the accident with April tomorrow, he didn't have to. He could just go and listen.

As I look back on the accident, and how Anders and I responded to it so differently, it's fascinating that our actions potentially affected us in the long term. For the first four weeks, I was visibly shaken by the events that took place. I had nightmares, cried constantly, and even suffered from panic attacks. It was concerning to all who were in my presence. But I worked through the trauma by putting my feelings into written and spoken words, sharing them often with family and friends. It felt almost therapeutic for me to tell my story, in spite of the emotional difficulties it caused. Eventually I was able to heal. Anders hid from his fears. He ignored the fact that it happened and never faced it. On the outside, it may have appeared that he was resilient and quick to recover. But on the inside, his terror was only growing, and consuming the happy, confident boy that he used to be. It was changing him emotionally and affecting him physically.

Moreover, my son dealt with the trauma of me leaving him at the scene. I'm sure there were all kinds of fears and emotions he experienced that I never knew or understood. His memories and pain would be unlike mine. He was his own person and would process them differently, simply because he was Anders and I was me. Our age could have also been a factor in how we each handled the experience. Someone as young as Anders may not know how to articulate their fears and understand emotions like an adult would.

Anders started therapy with April, seeing her several times a week. After only a few sessions, he began to respond positively to her methods of communication, breathing techniques and treatment. She diagnosed Anders with Post-Traumatic Stress Disorder due to the events of our van accident. PTSD usually begins within three months after a person has gone through or witnessed a traumatic event such as an assault, the sudden loss of a loved one, an accident, war or a natural disaster. Most people who experience a traumatic event will have reactions that may include shock, fear, nervousness, anger and even guilt. These reactions are common; and for most people, they go away over time. I could relate to this explanation as I dealt with such strong emotions myself for several weeks immediately following the accident. I cried all the time as I lived in a panicky state. Eventually though, my frantic frame of mind gradually subsided and I was able to get back into a normal way of living once again. But for a person with PTSD, these feelings linger and even increase, becoming so strong that they keep the person from living a normal life.

PTSD is a very real and debilitating condition, and I have gained the utmost respect for all who face it. Whether they are soldiers coming home from active military duty, women who've suffered a violent attack, or a person who has survived a natural disaster; I believe it can often take *more* courage to face the future after a traumatic event, than the actual incident itself. Traumatic memories, fears, survivor's guilt and depression are heavy burdens to bear on a daily basis. But I can attest that there is hope. I have both experienced and witnessed it. For us, hope has come from modern medicine, therapy, the body of believers, prayer, and most of all faith in Christ and the promise that He will never leave us or forsake us.

Sessions progressed as April used Trauma Focused Cognitive Behavioral Therapy with Anders. One day during a session, she told us that she had plans for him to create his very own book, telling the story of the accident in his own words. Anders looked skeptical as she explained further. April wanted him to first dictate the story in chronological order while she typed it out, and then finally, complete the project with illustrations. She warned me in private that this process could be lengthy and intense, especially with Anders' initial hesitancy to discuss the accident. But in the end, it should prove to be a very constructive and beneficial exercise. I had asked a few of our closest family and friends to pray that our son could eventually feel secure enough to share his story with his trusted doctor.

As the book project got under way, I remained in another office down the hall, giving Anders the privacy and space to share his side of the accident and not be hindered by any potential first impressions from me. This needed to be his side of the story alone. But once the book was completed, Anders would be able to present the finished product by reading it aloud to me. April also told Anders that when his story was all done, he could choose a special way to celebrate; maybe with a favorite dessert, doing something fun with a friend, or going somewhere with Mom and Dad. Anders didn't need much time to think about the prospect of a reward. He knew within minutes how we wanted to celebrate.

"I think I'd like to have a taco party! We can invite my friends, and Carson and Ella's friends too so we all can have fun and have people to play with." Anders announced with enthusiasm.

I was impressed by his idea and thoughtful gesture. Although, it did surprise me some; I honestly had no idea he liked tacos so much!

"Anders, that is a wonderful way to celebrate and we can definitely do that." I told him with reassurance. He felt very pleased with this arrangement. But he understood that he had some hard work ahead of him.

After the first couple sessions of book writing, April filled me in on how the assignment was going. That particular day, Anders had made incredible headway and she was almost giddy as she described his progress.

"Leanne, it was absolutely amazing! It was as if a wall came down and he finally felt the freedom to say what he had witnessed and experienced. I couldn't even type fast enough, he was telling the story so quickly; and I'm an efficient typist! It was as if he was just spilling out the words that had been bottled up inside him for so long." Anders looked quite proud as April boasted of his story-telling skills. "With the kind of progress we made today, we should have this book finished much sooner than I thought!" She said.

April was right. Instead of the estimated weeks it would take to have Anders tell and illustrate the story of the van accident, he was able to share it all in a matter of only a few sessions. And when the time came for him to present me with the finished book, he was extremely pleased. In fact, he was so proud; he wanted other family members to be present at the counseling session to hear him read his book.

"Why can't my sister and brother come; or my dad? I want them to see my book too." Anders asked April. But she was clear that this book was meant for only the three of us to see and that she would keep it in her office for safe keeping. Now that the book was finished, he could go on with his life being a happy, normal kid and not worry about the story of the van accident ever again. Although, he was certainly free to talk about it or tell others about his experience if he wanted to. Reluctantly, he agreed.

When the time came for him to show me his book and read it aloud, I sat in awe. Here was a boy who once was so stricken with fear; he literally went into hiding if anyone spoke of the accident. Nathan and I had watched him slowly crumble and let anxiety change the confident, outgoing, fun-loving boy he used to be. Now, he stood before me ready to let it all out and share the hurt and fear that was nearly bursting inside of him for months. I felt so much anticipation as he cleared his throat and began to tell his story.

"*The Accident*, by Anders Waterworth, ..." he began.

His book started out like any other typical seven-year-old's personal narrative by sharing facts about himself. "My name is Anders and I like pizza and football." I smiled and nodded my head in approval as he looked up from his paper to make sure I was paying close attention. But very soon his story took a very different turn. He wasted no time diving into a difficult narrative with facts about what happened on August 1, 2014. It was interesting to me the things that were important to him and what he took away from that day. He wrote about his shock immediately following the accident and me carrying him out of the van. In his story, he was very concerned about me having lost my shoes and phone in the creek. He remembered the neighbor lady cleaning the blood off of his face and giving him a lime popsicle, and later a grape one. He remembered watching the movie *Despicable Me 2* on an iPad while at the scene of the accident. And he also wrote how amazed he was to be so close to a real police car and helicopter. Such details! And the illustrations to go along with his account were remarkable too. Even though it was somewhat painful to look at his drawings, it was also therapeutic because I knew that all of this was helping Anders toward recovery. He needed to face this and then finally put it behind him.

The final paragraph reflected one of the valuable lessons he learned from April.

> *"My advice to other kids is if they are in a car accident or if they are in any kind of scary accident, they should not keep their worries in their brain because it can make you feel sick. Tell your mom or dad or grandpa or grandma or uncle or aunt so they can help you to take the worries out of your brain."*

As he closed the last page of his book, we saw a tangible end to this story and could begin to look forward to the rest of his life.

Today, more than two years after the accident, Anders is almost completely recovered from PTSD. He's had a few relapses but thanks to some additional treatment, and the reassuring presence of our loyal, yellow lab named Gunnar, who we used as a non-certified therapy dog, we are experiencing light at the end of what was a long, dark tunnel. Anders just wrapped up his first season of tackle football, and loved every second of it. There is hope!

> 1 Peter 5:10, *"And the God of all grace, who called you to his eternal glory in Christ, after you have suffered a little while, will himself restore you and make you strong, firm and steadfast."*

Final Words

As I write these final words, it's no coincidence that I'm doing so during the week of Thanksgiving. Today, the temperature is a chilly 30 degrees and a half inch layer of ice and snow covers the ground. Yesterday, as it fell from the sky and the arctic wind blew, I finally resigned myself to the fact that it was time to drag out my family's boots, snow pants, gloves, scarves, earmuffs, long underwear, and hats for the unavoidable winter season. I thought back to a time when this would have depressed me; but thankfully not anymore. God has done a miraculous work in my heart in so many ways and I am grateful that I can have peace and contentment, even when the snow flies.

Our family has gone through some extreme highs and lows, all within a two year period. The Lord showed us that it is possible to be thankful in the midst of it. In fact, I have learned *the most* about being thankful through the very darkest times in my life. I could have become bitter and resentful with the circumstances placed in our path. Instead, God revealed what is truly important: His grace, His presence, and His promises. From tick disease and flooded basements, to a double diagnosis of Cystic Fibrosis; it was in these places of distress and desperation that I felt God's existence and comfort the most. He loved us through it all!

I wouldn't wish these experiences on anyone, and yet in a strange way, Nathan and I feel blessed having gone through them because they remind us that life is fleeting and precious. Our growing children show us that indeed, the years fly by. And we never know what tomorrow may hold.

Personally, I have felt a sort of shaking in my spirit, especially since the van accident. The realization that we must make the most of each day and live as if it could be our last has become a foundation for my own personal mission statement. The Bible reminds us,

> James 4:14, *"Why, you do not even know what will happen tomorrow. What is your life? You are a mist that appears for a little while and then vanishes."*

Interestingly, when our boys were diagnosed with a life threatening illness, I assumed that someday, Cystic Fibrosis would be what takes their life. But after the van accident, I realized that only God knows what our future holds. The fact that Anders very easily could have died that day is something I will never ever forget. Every passenger in that vehicle had serious lacerations, injuries or broken bones. It's nothing short of a miracle. And not a day goes by that I don't look at him and say, "Thank you Jesus that I get to hold my son." I feel that way about all of my children. Every single day is a gift! I wish everyone could fully comprehend the enormousness of that truth.

We need to make the most of every opportunity, with every person we come into contact; whether it is family, friends, neighbors, coworkers, the cashier at the grocery store, and even motorists in traffic. Tell the ones you love how much they mean to you; don't just assume they know. Show people you care. Be kind. Say thank you! If need be, apologize; forgive. Bring someone flowers when they least expect it. It doesn't have to be their birthday. Make that phone call, send a text, or write a note, by hand even. Return an abandoned cart in a parking lot. Volunteer with youth. By doing these intentional acts of kindness, I promise, it will make your life richer, and someone else's too. Most importantly, you will please and glorify God. He desires us to live in this manner, with no regrets! With every breath you take, remember, there is always reason to choose joy and praise the One who loves you most.

Psalm 150:6, *"Let everything that has breath praise the Lord!"*

~ Update on our Family ~

Shortly after completing this manuscript, Carson, (age 14) and Anders, (age 9) went in for their 12 week check-ups at the University of Minnesota, Masonic Children's hospital. The boys endured thorough examinations and tests. The staff was pleased to report their pulmonary lung function and overall health remains in stable condition. We are so grateful for the life-saving medications, treatments, and care our boys receive.

We all remain active in the Cystic Fibrosis Foundation, Minnesota Chapter as volunteers and advocates. Our team, the CF Superheroes continues to have a presence at the Stair climb and Cycle for Life events. And for two years now, Anders' elementary school has allowed us to come in and put on a week of educating and fundraising on behalf of the CFF. We call it: *Cents for CF*. Our community rocks!

We keep in touch with Susan Imming and someday, we hope to visit the beautiful memorial that was created in Dan's honor at the Elk Creek Fire Station in Conifer, Colorado.

Our family continues to stay involved and be blessed by the Hopekids Organization. They asked us to participate in a promotional video, spotlighting the wonderful things that Hopekids does for families that have a child with a life threatening medical condition. You can find it at the HopeKids Inc. YouTube channel.

We remain connected with Mike and Holly, our wish grantors from Make-A-Wish, Wisconsin, and we also volunteer for the organization. One winter, the kids and I drove to Madison, Wisconsin, and participated in the *Z104 Make-A-Wish Radio-A-Thon*. We were invited to share our experiences during a live radio broadcast in an effort to raise awareness and funds for new wish experiences. It was really exciting and rewarding to feel like we could give back in some small way.

We've received so much encouragement and made unforgettable memories and friends from all of these organizations that are truly making a difference in the lives of others. Find out how you can get involved in The Cystic Fibrosis Foundation, Hopekids, and Make-A-Wish!

Cystic Fibrosis Foundation, Minnesota Chapter: 100 N 6th St #604a Minneapolis, MN 55403
Phone: (651)631-3290, www.cff.org/Minnesota

Hopekids, Minnesota Chapter: PO Box 44712, Eden Prairie MN 55344
Phone: (952)270-8271, www.hopekids.org

Make-A-Wish®, Wisconsin Chapter: 13195 West Hampton Avenue Butler, WI 53007
Phone: (262)781-4445, www.wisconsin.wish.org

Printed in the United States
By Bookmasters